A Country Music CHRISTMAS

A Country Music CHRISTMAS

CATHIE PELLETIER • PATSI BALE COX • JIM GLASER

WITH PHOTOGRAPHS BY CARL E. HILEMAN

Crown Publishers, Inc • New York

Grateful acknowledgment is made to Sony/ATV Music Publishing
for permission to reprint lyrics of "Old Toy Trains" by Roger Miller. © 1967 Sony/ATV Songs LLC (Renewed).
All rights administered by Sony/ATV Music Publishing, 8 Music Square West, Nashville, TN 37203.

Mama's Fried Taters recipe on page 144 reprinted with permission from *Stella Parton's Country Cookin'*.
Copyright © 1995 Adams Media Corporation.

Thanks to Jeanne Pruett for permission to reprint Sweet Potato Casserole on page 146 from her *Feedin' Friends* cookbook.

Recipe for Oatmeal Refrigerator Cookies on page 154 reprinted with permission of *Farm Journal*.

Published by Crown Publishers, Inc., 201 East 50th Street, New York, New York 10022.
Member of the Crown Publishing Group.
Random House, Inc. New York, Toronto, London, Sydney, Auckland
http://www.random house.com/
CROWN is a trademark of Crown Publishers, Inc.

Printed in the United States of America

Library of Congress Cataloging-in-Publication Data is available upon request

ISBN 0-517-70684-9
10 9 8 7 6 5 4 3 2 1
First Edition

In memory of

Sarah Ophelia Cannon

"Minnie Pearl"

1912–1996

Contents

BILL ANDERSON 15

Tomorrow I'll Have My Own Bike...

Remember the social importance of owning that very first bicycle? This story will surely make you smile. But it will also bring back that childhood anxiety: What if your dad can't afford it? What if—heaven forbid—the bicycle store burns down?!

JOHN BERRY 19

When The Family's Together, We're Blessed...

His earliest Christmases were spent in a rustic cabin, but now John celebrates the holidays at his own *Wolf Creek Farm*. Family unity means everything to John Berry, especially after a serious illness threatened to take it from him.

SUZY BOGGUSS 23

Santa Was So Sorry...

Coming from Illinois snow country, Suzy Bogguss was accustomed to ice skates, sleds, and hockey sticks. But her all-time favorite Christmas present had to do with a special Thumbelina doll, and a Santa Claus who was all thumbs!

GARTH BROOKS .27

You're Gonna See Your Mom...

The loyal dedication Garth Brooks feels toward his family lies at the heart of this story, when he and his wife, Sandy, are struggling against the weather to make it back to Oklahoma in time to celebrate Christmas.

JEFF CARSON 29

Mom Refers To Me As Grinch Carson...

Jeff Carson has had idyllic Christmases, thanks to a mom and dad who left city life behind and headed out for small-town America. His holiday tales are of the Purple Bomber, wooden Santas, and a Christmas song by Little Joe Cartwright!

I'd Volunteer To Work Overtime...

Christmas had become just another day to Aaron Tippin. He didn't celebrate; he worked overtime. Then, during an unforgettable trip to Saudi Arabia, with comedian Bob Hope, he discovered the true meaning of the season.

It Must Be Santa Coming Early...

The Tuckers had two Christmases, one on Christmas Eve and the other on Christmas morning. But one exciting holiday still stands out in Tanya Tucker's mind, and it started with a thump on the roof of the family's house trailer.

The Surprise Of My Life...

Even though he's known for his guitar-playing abilities, Steve Wariner never asked Santa for a Fender or a Gibson. His favorite Christmas presents involve G. I. Joe, a football, and something special that was waiting outside in his garage.

Christmas Had Become A Habit...

The extended family of aunts, uncles, and cousins was drifting apart, until a memorable evening brought them back together. And it all happened in Grandma White's kitchen, otherwise known as "Christmas Headquarters."

ACKNOWLEDGMENTS

Cathie Pelletier: For my mother and father, **Ethel O'Leary Pelletier** and **Louis Pelletier,** for making my childhood Christmases in northern Maine unforgettable. I carry images of pine cones and tassels, presents hidden in the cellar, a December moon on the river, and "The Apple Man," who always appeared at Christmastime, driving an old truck loaded with crates of oranges and apples. These memories are the greatest gifts you've given me. Thank you, **Skeeter Davis,** for your friendship, and your generous help in getting this book off the ground. It's so like you! **And our deepest thanks to the people who appear within these pages, for sharing their lives with us, and trusting us to tell their stories with heart and soul.**

Patsi Bale Cox: On Christmas Eve, 1985, my eighty-three-year-old mother, **Elizabeth Johnson Bale,** tried on her new holiday sweater, played games with her grandchildren, and, while a winter storm howled across the Kansas plains, mentioned that it had been ten long years since my father, **Charlie Bale,** passed away—ten years since they'd spent a Christmas together. That night she suffered a fatal, but painless, heart attack, and spent Christmas morning with her husband.

Jim Glaser: For my parents, **Marie Davis Glaser** (b. 1902–d. 1993) and **Louis N. Glaser** (b. 1901–d. 1979), who celebrated their first Christmas together in the sandhills of Nebraska.

Carl E. Hileman: For my grandfather **Tom Donahue** who sat with me on a southern Illinois porch swing, and told me all about his travels as a telegrapher for the G M & O Railroad. Tom Donahue passed away on Christmas Day, 1973. And to my parents, **Carl L.** and **Margaret Ann Hileman,** for always believing. For my son **Bryan,** and for **Sharon Hesselmeyer,** for sticking with me.

Special thanks to **Betty Prashker,** who first believed in this book, and to **Sharon Squibb,** a true-born Tennessean, who carried it forward. And **Lynne Amft,** the book designer, who labored long and hard, and **Lauren Dong,** the art director. And thanks to everyone at **Crown Publishers, Inc.,** for believing in **Nashville Books.** Thank you, **Allison Corlew,** our graphic artist, for working late, and for your indispensable sense of humor. And **Martha P. Trachtenberg,** our copyeditor.

Carl E. Hileman thanks the following people: Those good friends (some appear in the photos) who opened their homes at every time of night and day, and who stood on call for every whim: **Dave Prosser** (who also carved our Santas), **Glenda Prosser, Mark Glaab, Lisa Glaab, Amanda Cain, Kenneth Cain, Erin Cain, Casey Cain, Annette Stiff, Douglas Hileman,** and **Elizabeth Hileman.** And to my fellow photographers who aided me with friendship and advice: **Dan Overturf, Joe Garrett,** and **Chris Gauthier.** And to the folks who contributed items ranging from puppies to rare antiques: **Beverly Beasley, Denise LaMeer, Cathy Kirt, Joyce Mowery, Phil Hileman, Shelly Dowdy, Pansy Kirby, Mary Ward, Pam Bigham, Sharon Abercrombie,** and the **Village of Tamms, Illinois.**

Thanks to the **Joe Taylor Artist Agency** for their support and encouragement. And a final, special thanks to **Earl** and **Gerry O'Leary,** for the gift of **Augusta McKinnon O'Leary's** clock, which appears in the Skeeter Davis artwork. And to **Orcelia's Millinery,** for the Minnie Pearl hat.

Nashville's First Christmas

Christmas Day has always been an integral part of the colorful tapestry which makes up the history of Nashville, Tennessee. Tradition maintains that it was a cold winter's day, December 25, 1779, that early pioneer James Robertson led a party of nearly 400 exhausted followers—along with their horses, sheep, hogs, and cattle—across the frozen Cumberland River to a spot already known as French Lick. Here, on a bluff overlooking the river, was a salt lick and a sulfur spring, both enticements to the first lone travelers who passed through the wilderness there. One such woodsman was Jacques-Timothe De Montbrun, a trader born and raised in Trois-Rivières, Quebec, and now regarded as the "first citizen" of Nashville. But it was not until James Robertson came with a few hundred settlers that French Lick grew into Fort Nashborough and, finally, *Nashville.*

Over two hundred years have passed since James Robertson and his weary companions crossed the Cumberland River. Today, visitors will see signs announcing "Demonbreun Street," and "James Robertson Parkway." But very few tourists will know about Jacques-Timothe De Montbrun, the French-Canadian trader, or James Robertson, the dashing young frontiersman. These visitors have come to Tennessee's capital because it is known worldwide as the citadel of country music: *Music City U.S.A.*

It is to this facet of Nashville, Tennessee, to the stars of country music, that we look for the contents of this book. Their stories of Christmases past will entertain and delight you. But they will also serve to commemorate that first Christmas Day, in 1779, when James Robertson stood on a spot overlooking the icy Cumberland River, and saw in the distance a brave new dream, for a brave New Year.

Bill Anderson

"...firemen were called to Jenkins Cycle Shop..."

Columbia was a peaceful city when I was growing up, but it has had a turbulent past. During the American Revolution two major conflicts occurred on her soil, the Battle of King's Mountain, and the Battle of Cowpens. These were two startling victories, when you consider that untrained American frontiersmen defeated the well-trained British.

Later on, in 1865, when General William Tecumseh Sherman marched through Columbia, two-thirds of the city burned. There are still shell marks on the old stone building that is now the state legislature. But the only scars I remember from my boyhood days back in South Carolina were the ones I received in major bicycle wrecks. That brings me to the story of my first bike, and a holiday narrative that still remains fresh in my memory, even though many years have passed since it happened.

I must have been about ten years old the Christmas I nearly drove my parents crazy asking for a bicycle. When they had inquired as to what I might like under the tree on Christmas morning, I confessed to having a one-track, two-wheeled mind. I wanted that shiny blue Columbia-brand bicycle I had seen in the window at Jenkins Cycle Shop. I wanted nothing more, but I wasn't going to be happy with anything less. I simply *had* to have that bicycle.

We lived in a suburban, low-rise apartment project, replete with wide, inter-connecting concrete sidewalks, a safe, perfect place for a young boy and his buddies to ride. And every single one of my pals had his own bicycle. Everybody but me.

I knew my folks would do everything they could to make me happy on Christmas—

hadn't they always?—but I also knew my dad had just quit his longtime job and gone into business for himself. Money was tight. The future was uncertain. And bicycles didn't come cheap. The one I had my heart set on cost at least thirty dollars!

Nonetheless, I was excited. Deep down in my heart I just knew my folks wouldn't let me down. I was so pumped-up, so impatient for the big day to arrive, that by Christmas Eve I had become a nervous disaster.

I got up early that morning, borrowed Dickie Campbell's bike and pedaled around the apartment complex for hours. Then, when he wanted it back, I borrowed Mike Barron's and rode some more. "This time tomorrow I'll have my *own* bicycle," I boasted, all the time nursing a queasy, taunting feeling deep in the pit of my stomach that seemed to whisper, "It ain't gonna happen, boy, it ain't gonna happen."

By three o'clock Christmas Eve afternoon I was exhausted. I stumbled back to our small apartment to try and relax. I fell across my bed and flipped on my tableside radio. I thought perhaps I could find some live country music. But it wasn't to be. Instead of the songs of Tommy Trent and the Dixie Fun-Barn Gang, or some of my favorites from the famed WSB *Barn Dance*, I heard the anxious voice of our local announcer: *Firemen have just been called to Jenkins Cycle Shop on Church Street where a giant blaze is threatening to destroy the building.* My heart sank.

Mom and Dad had gone to a Christmas open house at the home of some friends and wouldn't be back until after dark. My only sister, Mary, was visiting a friend. I was home alone with no one to talk to, no one with whom to share my anxiety. My imagination immediately got busy painting all sorts of depressing pictures. I could just see my beautiful blue bicycle reduced to a pile of charred, smoking rubbish. I could almost smell the putrid odor emanating from the scalded rubber tires. It was about to be the most depressing Christmas anyone had ever been forced to endure.

There was nothing I could do but stay put and nervously wait. I made myself a peanut butter and jelly sandwich. I went outside. I came back in. It grew dark so I turned on the lights on our Christmas tree. It didn't make things festive. It only made things worse. I yanked the plug and the lights went back off again. I walked upstairs. I came back down, all the time wondering: How bad had the fire been? Was everything in the building a total loss? Had anyone been hurt? More specifically and much more importantly to me, had my big blue bicycle—the one I just knew my dad had bought for me—been destroyed?

It seemed like forever, but it was only a few minutes past eight o'clock when I finally looked out my bedroom window and saw the headlights from my parents' returning car. Dad eased the two-door black 1941 Chevy into the driveway, backed up, maneuvered forward, and glided the old car into its assigned parking place. Then he opened the door on the driver's side and got out.

When the door opened, the dome light inside the car came on and I saw it. It lay at an angle, resting awkwardly in the tiny space between the front seat and the back. At first I saw only the handlebars, then one of the tires. Then, before Dad could close the door and come inside, I feasted my eyes on the body of the most gorgeous, shiny blue bicycle that ever existed in the civilized world. I raised my arms in triumph. My bike had survived the fire. I was going to get my Christmas wish after all.

The next morning I tried to act surprised. Dad said solemnly, "They had a real bad fire at Jenkins' yesterday afternoon. There were over fifty bicycles in the store at the time. Yours must have been parked close to the door. It was one of only eight they were able to save." I was thrilled, but I wasn't so excited that I didn't hurt for the other forty-plus kids who had been wanting and expecting bicycles for Christmas just like me. I knew those kids must be terribly disappointed. I tried imagining myself in their place, but the thought was too painful to hold.

I hugged my mom and dad, hopped on "Bluey" (it didn't take long for me to give my new pride and joy a name) and roared off down the sidewalk. I knew boys my age weren't supposed to believe in Santa Claus, but I wasn't so sure. Santa Claus—or somebody an awful lot like him—had sure been mighty good to me!

John Berry

AIKEN, SOUTH CAROLINA

"...we were in the woods, and we had BB guns..."

When I was eight years old we moved into a log cabin on the outskirts of my hometown of Aiken, South Carolina. It was an old two-story cabin, built in 1928, and the only heat we had was from the fireplaces. That Christmas my brother and I got BB guns, just like in the movie, *The Christmas Story*. For the adults, living in a cabin far from town, with no heating system, must have been something of a hardship. But for my brother and me that Christmas was pure heaven: We were in the woods, and we had BB guns. Not long ago I drove out there just to see it again. I could picture two little boys creeping through the woods with their guns, great woodsmen and hunters.

Now my wife, Robin, and I, and our three children celebrate Christmas at home in Pocataligo, Georgia, which is about eighteen miles north of Athens. We call it *Wolf Creek Farm*, and, yes, we do have a pet wolf. It's a family enclave with my mother-in-law living next door. We're still out in the woods, but we do have a few more amenities than when we lived in the cabin! We don't have to heat the house with fireplaces, but it wasn't until last year that we had a paved driveway. The road up to our place is steep, and it's four hundred and eighty feet long. That can get pretty tough to navigate when it rains hard, so last year I decided that what I really wanted was a paved road.

Because my tour schedule is so hectic, I take most of December off to be with my family and friends. Robin and I started a holiday tradition in 1988, the year we got married. With help from Robin's sister-in-law, Traci, we performed an acoustic Christmas show at Green Acres Baptist Church, which we attend in Athens. Members asked us to perform the

19

following year, and from then on the show has just continued to grow and take on a life of its own. Several of my band members got involved, including a fiddle player who can play wonderful hymns on the violin. Members of the University of Georgia orchestra called one year, and they, too, joined our group. We added lights and additional sound equipment, and the show has now become so well-attended that we do two concerts each Christmas. I can't imagine anything ever stopping us from making that concert. It's the most important show I do all year. I'm sure everyone feels this way about the people in their home church, but the congregation at Green Acres is made up of some of the most wonderful people I've ever met. Somehow, coming back and being with these people during the holidays gives me a strength and spirituality that I carry with me throughout the year, no matter where I am.

My family has our big Christmas dinner on Christmas Eve afternoon. We have a very traditional meal, with turkey, ham, sweet potato pie, and several absolutely required dishes like corn bread dressing (it *has* to be corn bread), real macaroni and cheese (never from a box!), cranberry and orange salad, and my personal favorite, pecan pie.

Then, on Christmas Eve, Robin's brothers come with their families, and we have our annual hayride, which has also become a tradition with the family. We load up a hay wagon with hay, hook it up to the tractor, and everyone piles on, family and friends alike. We pull it out to a nearby field, build a huge fire, sing carols, and roast marshmallows. My brother-in-law, Mark, reads the Christmas story. Then we go around the circle, with each of us sharing the things that we are most thankful for during the past year.

The song "I'll Be Home for Christmas" has a special meaning for us because Robin's brothers are military officers. At any given moment they might be called to a part of the world where Christmas in Georgia would become an impossibility. The song also has a very deep, personal meaning for me, Robin, and our children. Life can change drastically from one holiday to another, and we learned just how much a couple of years ago. During the Christmas season of 1993 we were very excited because we had our first taste of chart success and believed we'd finally made that all-important career breakthrough. Things appeared to be perfect, especially since Robin was pregnant with our second child. But right after Christmas that year I began to change. I grew depressed and I started suffering from memory lapses and headaches. Robin was fearful that something was wrong with our marriage, and I know how hard those months were on her.

I had been on tour with Reba McEntire and hadn't even been close to a doctor until I came off tour in late April to be with Robin during the baby's birth. I was sitting on the floor in the hospital hallway, head in hands, when a nurse stopped and asked me if something was wrong. I finally had to admit that something seemed *very* wrong. After running some tests, the doctors found a cyst located at the base of my brain, and scheduled me for surgery. Thankfully, the operation went well and I ultimately made a complete recovery.

My first public appearance after the operation was at Fan Fair in Nashville. When I walked out on the stage and those twenty thousand wonderful fans cheered for me, my emotions were so strong that I almost started crying. After I performed, my friend Charlie Daniels came out, gave me a huge bear hug, and we both broke down and wept.

It wasn't always easy in those next months, though. I forgot lines to songs and tired easily. Some concerts had to be cancelled. But during the time I was in the hospital I did have my first number one song, "Your Love Amazes Me." And, when I consider what she went through during that time, Robin's love *still* amazes me.

The very next Christmas we stood out in the field and listened as the story of Christmas was read. Then we all began giving thanks. For me it was a *big* thanks, because in the months between these two Christmas celebrations, our lives had been turned upside down, then righted again. But there we were. We were all healthy. We had our wonderful new baby. And we were all together. That's the thing we've tried to teach our children. Every time the family can all be there for Christmas together, we are blessed.

Suzy Bogguss

ALEDO, ILLINOIS

"...Santa dropped Thumbelina, and she broke..."

Living in Aledo, Illinois, was much like a 1950s television show. We led truly All-American lives in that little, rural town. We were about seven miles from the Mississippi River, just close enough to develop a love for the Big River, but far enough away to keep us from being the River Rats we'd like to have been. In some parts of the U.S. the Mississippi borders on cotton fields. But in my part of the country, the river bordered flat fields of tall corn. When people ask me to spell *Aledo* for them I always get the urge to shout A-L-E-D-O and then follow it with a big "Hip, hip hooray." This is because I'm a former high school cheerleader!

People come back to Aledo. It's not a town where the population dwindles year after year. When I was in school we had a population of over three thousand, and we still do. That little town just seems to regenerate itself. I guess people there know the benefits of living in such a closely-knit community.

Since Aledo is in snow country, many of my childhood Christmases involved gifts like ice skates, sleds, hockey sticks, and heavy snow wear like mittens, caps, and parkas. Christmastime was always family and community time. Friends dropped in throughout the holidays. My mother's family lived twenty miles away and my father's parents lived thirty or forty miles from Aledo. Most of the time, the grandparents came to our house for the festivities. Although the aunts and uncles and cousins didn't actually spend Christmas day with us, we always visited more often during the holidays. We spent a great deal of time getting the house decorated for the season, and decorating became a sore spot for me.

There is a positive side and a negative side to being the baby of the family. The up side was that everyone wanted things perfect for the "baby." The down side was that they didn't think I was mature enough to help decorate. "You can't just throw big globs of icicles on the tree!" they'd say. "You have to put them on one by one!" I was far too impatient for that.

One of my most anticipated, hoped-for, and dreamed-about gifts was a Thumbelina doll, back when I was around ten years old. It was a very trendy doll and my mother spent weeks searching for it, since every other mother in Illinois was also on its trail. Finally, she found one, brought it home, and was preparing to wrap it the night before Christmas. Being so proud of having located the elusive Thumbelina, Mother decided to wait until she could show it off to my aunt. When my aunt arrived, Mother wound the crank on Thumbelina's back so that my aunt could see how the doll actually moved. But as Mother wound Thumbelina up, the crank broke completely off. I'm sure she must have felt like dying at that moment. But being fast on her feet, she had a story all ready for me the next morning. "Santa was so sorry," she said, "but he accidentally dropped Thumbelina's box out of the sleigh, and she broke. He told me how to get her fixed, though. So I'm sending her back to him and he'll take care of it." I bought the whole story, and wasn't even disappointed since it meant that Santa had paid special attention. Plus, is there anything better than the smell of a new doll? Sometimes, even today, when I smell certain plastics, I remember Thumbelina. Mother sent her back to the North Pole (translate, *the factory*) and she came back good as new. Just like Santa promised. I still have Thumbelina, even though she has gone through many transformations, including hair transplants. After one too many hairdo makeovers I ruined her original hair. She was my fashion guinea pig, and after a time all her hair just rotted and fell out. I solved her doll–pattern baldness problem by cutting the locks off my "Beauty Parlor" doll and gluing them onto Thumbelina's head. The women in my family have always been problem solvers!

Our two greatest wishes each year were that we would enjoy a white Christmas, and that the family would all be healthy and happy and together. One year those wishes collided head-on. My grandparents had moved to California, and they were taking a train across country to spend the holidays in Aledo. Snow warnings were all over the news, and we were holding our breaths that nothing would go wrong. The idea of my grandparents stranded somewhere on a snowbound train on Christmas Eve was horrifying. But they arrived safe and sound on Christmas Eve, with not a drop of snow in sight. We all went to bed with a sigh of relief and awakened on Christmas morning to one of the heaviest snows the area had seen in years. Of course, all the stores were closed and nothing moved that morning. We watched this unbelievably peaceful scene and offered thanks that we were all snowbound, healthy and happy and together.

Since I was by far the baby of the family, with eight years separating me from my brother, the family made every effort to keep the magic of the season alive for me. I understand the importance of seeing Christmas through a child's eyes now more than ever since my own baby son was born last year. As time goes by we sometimes get caught up in the rush of the season. We hate standing in lines, fighting the traffic and crowds while in search of that elusive, "perfect" gift. In some ways, we spend too much effort making the rituals happen, and not enough time simply enjoying the season. But Christmas is once again magic when you watch a little child look at a manger scene or at brightly decorated store windows. Since my siblings are older than I, their children are already teenagers. So my baby, Ben, will change the face of our holiday season for them when we celebrate next year. They're excited. The grandparents are excited. As a matter of fact, my husband and I were so excited that we wrote a song about children and Christmas after Ben was born. It's called "Christmas Through Your Eyes," and it's about the thrill of having a child to once again remind us that Christmas is about love.

Garth Brooks

YUKON, OKLAHOMA

"...it was just like magic..."

Christmas is my favorite holiday, one that I've managed to spend with my family for each of my thirty-four years. The best Christmas I remember was in 1987. When Sandy and I moved to Nashville that year, we had never even been out of Oklahoma before. Our days were spent trying to find jobs and get my career going. By Christmas, we were desperate to see our folks. So we packed up our car—an old Monte Carlo Sandy's parents had given her—and we started for home.

By the time we reached Tulsa we were traveling through a mixture of rain and snow. When the sun went down that rain turned to ice. We spent the night in a motel, hoping the roads would clear some by morning. But the next day the sky was overcast and the roads were worse; they were thinking of closing Turner Turnpike. We decided to try our luck anyway, but twenty minutes after we started driving, we heard on the radio that they'd closed the turnpike. There wasn't any way to get across the median, so we had to keep moving. When it finally became too hazardous, we pulled over and just sat there by the roadside. There was nothing we could do. And we were certain that we wouldn't spend Christmas with our families.

Then it was just like magic! The sun came out and started melting the ice. It was slow, but the car could move again. When we were two blocks from home, Sandy turned to me and said, "Garth, you're gonna see your mom for Christmas." I don't remember any gifts I got that year, but I do remember driving those last few blocks home with tears in my eyes.

Jeff Carson

GRAVETTE, ARKANSAS

"...I had carved enough Santas for everyone..."

I guess my very best Christmas as a kid had to be when I was in the third grade, and not only got my first bike, but starred in the school's Christmas pageant. The bike was something to see. It was huge, at least to an eight-year-old, and painted purple with little sparkles that literally shimmered when I rode down the street and the sunlight caught it. Even the banana-shaped seat was purple. I went nuts when I saw that bike, and one of my first moves was to clothespin playing cards to the spokes. In case nobody saw The Purple Bomber coming, they could hear it for sure.

It would be hard to say whether I was more excited about the bike, or making my acting debut. My class in school put on *How the Grinch Stole Christmas,* and I was the lucky kid chosen to play the Grinch. Now, playing the Grinch may not be big-time show business, but it was a start. Mom worked for weeks making me a Grinch suit, and I practiced those lines so much around the house that to this day my mother sometimes refers to me as *Grinch Carson.* I can still recite most of the lines, too.

Back then we were living in Tulsa, Oklahoma, where I was born. One of the first things we'd do every year as the holidays rolled closer was go to the city library and rent *Christmas on the Ponderosa,* featuring songs and holiday stories from the Cartwrights, Ben, Hoss, and Little Joe. We loved that record, and I especially loved a song titled, "Santa Got Lost in Texas," one that Little Joe sang. I always hated the fact that nobody but me and my family had heard the song, so I spread it around whenever I got the chance.

Our whole family was musical, so Christmas found us singing and playing a good portion of the time. One grandpa played harmonica, and the other played fiddle and man-dolin. Harmonica became the first instrument I learned, and I loved it, since it was so easy for a kid. You can put your mouth on the harmonica and start in playing, even if not very well! My mother, Virginia, played banjo and guitar. We did "simplified" versions of Christmas songs, though. You'd be surprised at the number of chord changes in some of them.

We usually went to our grandparents' house on Christmas Eve, to see the aunts and uncles and cousins, then had our immediate family's Christmas the next morning. My first memory of this system was when I was a very little kid and couldn't quite understand about the two gift exchanges. We had a room of wrapped presents at home, and I guessed a lot of them would be for me. But then we went over to my grandparents' house, and the only gifts opened were a few things from relatives. It wasn't precisely what I'd expected the Christmas gift-giving thing to be about. When we piled in the car to go home, I started sniffling in the back seat. Mom asked me what in the world was the matter. I said, "Well, I only got six presents!" They set me straight about how it worked right then. They also set me straight about how lucky we all were to be able to exchange gifts. My older brother, Steve, and my sister Karen didn't let me forget it either, even though I later tried to pass it off as just a "baby of the family" sort of misunderstanding.

Both my parents were Tulsa natives, graduates of Tulsa University, and people who seemed like candidates for lifelong residency there. My father, Clyde, had a good, solid job in a bank and life looked pretty well set. Then my grandmother Carson moved to Gravette, Arkansas, to be close to her sister and we visited her there. Gravette is a tiny town, population fourteen hundred or so, in northwest Arkansas. It's a laid-back little place with lots of trees, streams, and wooded areas, in addition to some open plains. Mom and Dad couldn't get the town out of their minds. The more Dad went to work at the bank in downtown Tulsa, the more he thought about what life might be like in Gravette.

I was still in grade school when my folks decided to change their lifestyle. And what a change it was for Dad, from city banker to rural hog farmer and school bus driver. We lived on eighty-five acres in Arkansas, and between the hogs, planting a huge garden, and both my folks driving school buses, Mom used to say we were living out the *Green Acres* scenario. I loved the change as much as they did, and I consider Gravette my true home-town. I appreciated the fact that everybody knew everybody, that if a neighbor needed help, you jumped in and helped, and that the entire school system, elementary through junior high, was about the size of the grade school I'd attended in Tulsa. Now I love look-ing in my high school yearbook and knowing where people are, and how they are.

None of us have ever regretted the move. We never looked back. Dad is retired now, and he still has that garden. Mom works as the janitor at the middle school. Not many jobs for a former college girl there in Gravette, but she likes what she does and she does it well.

We brought the Carson family Christmas with us, so that was one thing that changed very little. We still played music and we still sang those Ponderosa songs, even though we didn't have anyplace to rent the record. Now that my sister and brother both have chil-dren, there's a whole new generation to fill with the holiday spirit. We always have the same traditional holiday meal—that one every other family probably has—turkey, dress-ing, and all the fixings. One thing all the kids look forward to is Mom's famous holiday breakfast, homemade biscuits and gravy. There's never a problem getting us up on Christ-mas morning for the presents, or any morning that Mom's baking biscuits.

About four years ago, I fulfilled a sneaking little desire I've always had: I would per-sonally make my gifts for the family. I'd always been fascinated with woodcarving, so I bought a bunch of cedar four-by-fours and started teaching myself to carve. Since the carv-ings were for Christmas, I decided to try my hand at Santas. Over a period of several months I got better and better, and by Christmas I had carved enough Santas for everyone in my family. I even made enough for my wife Kim's family, too. It was great to watch them open those presents, then offer comments like, "You really made this? Noooo!"

I fulfilled another little holiday dream last year. My producer, Chuck Howard, called me up and said, "Jeff, I think you should record a couple of Christmas songs to send out to radio. Have you got any favorites you'd like to do?" I don't know what songs he expected me to say, but I know for a fact he wasn't expecting "Santa Got Lost in Texas," by Little Joe Cartwright. Now, I have my own version. It helps a lot when I can't make it to the Tulsa Public Library during the holidays.

Skeeter Davis

...Santa had run out of toys...

My Christmas memories go back to the days of coal oil lamps and candles. We children went with Daddy to cut the Christmas tree. We'd look until we found a perfect cedar growing somewhere on the farm. I love the smell of cedar to this day. Sometimes, we'd make paper ornaments from pages of the catalogue, and then put strings through them for hanging. I do remember we had store-bought bulbs. And we strung popcorn to go around the tree. There were beads, and a lot of icicles. We used to have angel hair, and it seemed like that angel hair went a long way when it came to decorating. I don't know what year it was that we finally got bubble lights. These were little glass tubes filled with liquid that bubbled when the light was turned on. On Christmas Eve we'd be anticipating the arrival of Santa Claus. As the oldest child, my job was to get all the younger kids to sleep so that things could calm down. The next morning we got to see what Santa left under the tree.

The Christmas I was eight years old stands out most in my memory. We lived in an old log cabin down this country road in Dry Ridge, Kentucky. It was just a little country lane, not paved or anything. Sometimes, during wet periods, it would be just mud. Back in those days we didn't wrap presents, and there were no individual gifts. We all shared what was under the tree. It was only at Christmas that we had fruit and nuts and candy. There were apple trees on the farm, and peach trees, and pear trees, but we children weren't supposed to eat off those trees. That fruit was used for canning, and making apple cobblers and peach cobblers. Those trees represented food for the family, so we couldn't go get us an apple or peach when we wanted a treat. We were actually told, "Don't get in those trees.

Don't climb those fruit trees." So, this particular Christmas came and one of the presents Santa Claus left was a Red Flyer wagon, a little red wagon with a small railing around it. I can't remember for certain, but Daddy might have even made the railing. What I do remember was that the wagon was filled with apples and oranges and nuts and candy.

I can still see that Red Flyer wagon every time I think of that Christmas. I do remember one time that we got fruit on an occasion other than Christmas, and that's when my sister Carolyn was born. I remember that Daddy brought some grapes home to us. I thought that was so exciting. It was a big celebration. That's the only time I remember getting fruit, other than at Christmas.

When I was ten years old I wanted a doll. Instead of getting the doll I found a note left by Santa Claus saying that he'd run out of toys and that he was really sorry. He hoped I would understand. Everybody thought it was great that I'd gotten a note from Santa. But I went to the barn and lay down on the hay and cried my heart out. I felt like I was the only child in the world who didn't get a present from Santa Claus. I know there was a positive side. I did get that note. But to be honest, my heart was broken. The very next Christmas, I got the doll. What a great feeling! But I was also told that it would be the last doll. I collect dolls to this day. I've got them all over my house. I'm sure my interest in doll collecting goes back to that one Christmas.

I truly believed that our presents came from Santa Claus. I never did think that Mother and Daddy bought the gifts, so I never tried to spy, or find where gifts were hidden. Nobody ever sat me down and said otherwise. And I did get that letter from Santa saying that he hoped I was a big enough girl to understand why there was no doll. Nobody in the family ever dressed up like Santa Claus. And in those days you didn't see a Santa Claus on every street corner, like you do now. I think that's why it was easy to believe. So, I still believe in Santa Claus to this day, and don't tell me any different.

During the holidays we sang Christmas carols such as "Away in a Manger." I loved that song because I could relate to those words: *Away in a manger, no crib for His bed, the little Lord Jesus lay down His sweet head.* There we were on the farm, with hay, with that whole scene. And then, I've loved Jesus from an early time in my life, so I was fascinated with the story of Jesus being born on Christmas day. When I thought of Santa Claus bringing presents, I always remembered the three wise men traveling to bring gifts to Jesus.

In those days we couldn't afford Christmas cards. As a result I became a fanatic card-sender for years. I mailed Christmas cards to anybody who ever sent me a note. Nowadays, because of time and scheduling, I've gotten away from that. But when I was growing up, Christmas cards just weren't a big deal. In rural areas you often saw the people you knew, and you greeted them personally. The community always had church plays and school plays, and I participated in them regularly. I sang from an early age, so I got to sing little Christmas carols. I played Mary once. I always thought the reason they let me do it was because my real name is Mary Frances Pennick. They didn't have as many Christmas functions then as they do now. But I remember special people, like the relief workers who brought Christmas to the poor children who wouldn't have one otherwise. That's why there were songs like "When Santa Came to Shanty Town." It was an Eddy Arnold record from the early forties. I used to sing that song a lot because I could identify with it.

Everything we ate for Christmas dinner came off the farm. The fruit that we weren't allowed to pick in the summer became a cobbler, or some sort of dessert. The ham and turkey were raised on the farm. And then there were mashed potatoes, green beans, corn, and dressing. I didn't know what cranberry sauce was until later on. We always formed a family circle, with everybody holding hands while Daddy led the family in prayer. Sometimes it was a brother or sister who said the blessing. None of us were shy about saying our prayers out loud. It was always done.

Back when we were growing up we always had a white Christmas. You could just depend on it. The first day of May meant you would take your shoes off and go barefoot. And then, you put your shoes back on in September. Come November, there would be snow on the ground. I'm sure an old *Farmer's Almanac* would verify this. Nowadays, the weather has changed. But back then, you could count on a white Christmas. I remember that we used to make lots of snow angels. And it seemed like we didn't get sick then.

We didn't have ice cream so we made "snow cream." We'd get a kettle of snow and put milk and sugar and vanilla in it to make ice cream. So, I remember snow always being around, and it helped further my belief in Santa Claus and his reindeer. And I still remember the sounds of the bells we rang at Christmas. It seems like you rang bells just for the sound of them. We had cow bells and goat bells that were ordinarily used on the goats and sheep. This may not have qualified under "make a joyful noise," but those were the bells we used! We didn't get to play with those bells, or make all that racket, at any other time of the year. The sound of Christmas bells echoing across the snow is unforgettable.

I've just remembered, just this instant, a special gift that I got when I was a junior in high school. At that time, I had gone through quite a few Christmases without getting a present. I had spent the evening babysitting for our neighbors, who were Catholic and had gone to midnight Mass. When I got home my daddy had a present for me. "Well, it's already Christmas," he said. "Would you like to open your present?" I said no, that I preferred to wait until morning. But Daddy was so thrilled about it that Mother said, "Y'all go on and open your present." So, I did. It was a Gruen wristwatch, a little white gold wristwatch with a narrow black band which I still have to this day. I guess Daddy figured I was growing up and needed it.

Another wonderful Christmas for me was in 1969. I was divorced and living alone at this time. I had just come back from a nice European tour—England, Germany, and Scotland. But it was Christmastime, and I was lonely. I don't have children myself, so I called my sister Shirley. She had eight kids who were all Santa Claus age at the time. "Shirley," I said, "you've got to come to Nashville for Christmas. I just can't stand this being alone." So she and her husband came down from Kentucky. Shirley and I did all the shopping. We hid presents all over the house. I moved the furniture out of the living room and we put a big Norwegian pine tree in there and decorated it. That was one of the best Christmases that I've ever had. Just seeing those children was really, really wonderful.

Naturally there's some sadness connected with memories of the holidays because of just being poor. But not having money is not so bad when you live around other people who don't have money either. There was always a bit of sadness at Christmastime when my mother would drink. Her depression used to bleed off on me and, as the oldest child, I tried to keep everybody in a good mood by singing songs and entertaining the kids. But I always fell into a little bit of the sadness with Mother. After thinking in depth about this, I discovered why my mother was so melancholy. The last time she saw her father alive was on Christmas, when I was two years old. But I don't think about that any more. I'm only sorry that I didn't find out sooner. I might have helped her.

My parents had been in my life since day one, and losing them gave me a whole new perspective. The first Christmas after Mother was gone, the Christmas of 1983, the family didn't celebrate. I didn't even put up a tree. I know I didn't put my manger scene out because the children across the street said, "Miss Davis, when are you gonna put baby Jesus out there? When are you gonna put your manger out?" So, ever since then it's been out there, even though my daddy died in 1989, and my sister Susan passed away in 1990. I put the manger scene up a couple weeks before Christmas and leave it up the whole month of January. And I turn my outdoor lights on every night. I don't buy cut trees anymore, but I put up an artificial one that reaches all the way to the ceiling. To this day I've managed to keep bubble lights on my tree.

Several years ago my husband, Joey, gave me a Christmas angel for the top of the tree. It's all lit up, and it moves its wings. It's just beautiful. A lot of people say I have the prettiest Christmas trees, and I'm always tickled about that. My friends tease me, but I leave my tree up until Valentine's Day. The first time I did this Archie Campbell offered to come over and help me take down my decorations. He thought I was sick. "No, Archie," I told him. "I'm just not ready for Christmas to be over."

Even though I believe that Christmas has become too commercial—it even starts before Thanksgiving!—I have happy Christmases. And now God brings only those good memories from the past to my mind. Every season I love to buy gifts for my family members and fans. I've done this ever since I've been able to afford it. It's wonderful being Santa Claus. So, until I find out there isn't one, I'll continue to celebrate, and to share the joys of Christmas. But you know, looking back, it's really hard to think of any incident that was sad, for family is the most important thing. Back then all the kids were together. We had Mother and Daddy still with us, a few apples and oranges, and a little red wagon full of Christmas candy. What else could we have wanted?

Emilio

SAN ANTONIO, TEXAS

"...we hang the Christmas piñata..."

Christmas is a big, exciting party for the Navaira family. Everybody is home and everybody is having fun. One of the things that makes it such a wonderful holiday is that we all still live in the city where generations of us were born, San Antonio, and when I say *all* I mean a lot of folks! I come from a big family and so does my wife, Cindy. Luckily, all of us love San Antonio. We wouldn't leave even if they tried to kick us out! I've not missed any Christmases at home, even though Christmas shows are very profitable for an entertainer. But that's the way my mother and her mother and her mother before her raised us: Christmas is the most special and spiritual day of the year, one devoted to family.

Music is another important part of our tradition. We sing both Spanish songs and the traditional Christmas carols. Ever since I was nine years old and my brother and sister and I received a piano, we have gathered at the piano to sing and celebrate on Christmas Eve. I sincerely believe in giving children gifts that are shared. They learn so much when material things are viewed as something for all to enjoy. Cindy and I believe that this is the strongest tradition we are passing on to our boys, Emilio and Diego: the love of sharing what one has with family.

On Christmas morning we hang up the Christmas piñata, which is filled with little wrapped toys that we've collected and carefully wrapped. Again, the piñata is a way for the children to share in the season. They dance and sing and soon they are showered with gifts, much in the same way that we are all feeling showered with the love of Christmas.

Donna Fargo

MOUNT AIRY, NORTH CAROLINA

"...it was for me from my brother Gayle..."

My childhood years were spent seven miles from Mount Airy, North Carolina, where you will find the world's largest open-face quarry, which supplies our nation with tombstones. But that's not my hometown's only claim to fame. It's also the hosiery capital and the toaster capital of the world! During my growing-up years I often heard about how Mount Airy was the hometown of Andy Griffith. I never met him. He had already left by the time I went to Mount Airy High School. But all the townspeople took pride in the fact that our town had produced someone so famous, someone who had gone on, as my grandma would say, to "be somebody."

It was sometimes lonely out in the country. I remember sitting on the front porch, counting the few cars that passed, and dreaming of one day seeing the world. There were many nights that I spent just staring out at the moon from my bedroom window. As a young child I used to work in the tobacco fields. Tobacco was a big deal in this part of the country. Almost everybody raised it or worked in it. Not the people who lived in town, but country people. I remember helping my step-grandma in the barn. I would stand on an orange crate and hand the tobacco to her to tie on the stick. During those times it was just Grandma and me against the world. Sometimes we'd stay up all night guarding the barn and minding the fire as the tobacco was curing. We'd roast wieners and drink Pepsi-Colas. Grandma would encourage me. She said that I was going to "be somebody" someday. I loved Grandma Maud. We were definitely buddies. She and my mother and I would take trips together. Mother would get us up in the middle of the night and say, "Pack your bags.

Let's go to Florida." I was ready to go anywhere that southern wind happened to blow.

Christmas was a special time around our house. Our goal was to have presents for everyone who happened to stop by. We always had a collection of little gifts that anyone might want. In drastic cases, I'd sneak a package out of the room and change the tag. I sometimes wrapped up mini-packages of cigarettes for the smokers who came, putting five in each little box. We didn't want anyone to go away empty-handed, and I know that this tradition is one that began with my mother. She was such a good-hearted woman. She gave people things like a particularly pretty flower she'd planted, or a nice fabric she had on hand. Often she would buy fabrics in Virginia, and bring them back to sell. But she always gave away as much as she sold. At Christmas, she was really in her element! It didn't matter to our family how big the present was, and I, for one, didn't even care if it was new. I can remember going through my dad's tie rack and finding ties he hadn't worn in years, then wrapping them up. If he realized he already owned the tie, he never let on.

The element of surprise was very important at our house, especially with my brother Gayle. Gayle was wild, energetic, and played with the law. He liked to drive fast cars. He used to stay out all night with his friends on Christmas Eve, then he'd want to exchange gifts when he got home early Christmas morning. That worked until I got to be about eight years old and began to wonder why I had to wait so long. After all, Christmas morning came one minute past midnight, didn't it?

The year that I dreamed up the "minute-past-midnight" theory, we had even more presents than usual. I knew I could expect a doll from my dad, usually one that had a recording inside and you could wind it up and make it talk. My mother always got me pretty things to wear. But this year something different was sitting under the tree: the biggest package I'd ever seen, and it was for me from my brother Gayle. I had no idea what it could be. The longer I waited the more impatient I became. I thought of little else during those days before Christmas. Day after day that huge present stared at me.

A few minutes after midnight on Christmas Eve I couldn't wait any longer. The house was dark, so I slipped past the room where my parents slept. Then, I turned on a light and opened Gayle's present. It was a beautiful hope chest, and I was just the girl to fill it because I had enough hopes for lots of people. I was so excited! Not only did I have a fine hope chest, it had come from my big brother. I went off to bed, thrilled with myself.

The next morning when Gayle got in, he came right away to my room to wake me up and get started on Christmas. "I can't wait to see your face when you open my present," he said. "Oh, thank you for the hope chest!" I said, sleepily. "I love it!" Gayle was visibly stunned. "You *opened* it?" he asked. "Right after midnight," I said. "I just couldn't wait." Tears actually came to my brother's eyes when he realized he hadn't been a part of the surprise he'd planned so long for me. It dawned on me then just what I'd done. I had stolen his joy at seeing the spontaneous wonder and surprise when that thoughtfully and carefully chosen present was opened. Instead of *giving* that Christmas, I had selfishly *taken*.

I learned one of the most important lessons of my life that Christmas morning. You must always be aware of other's feelings and often put them before your own. So, I made myself a promise, one that I carried with me, long after I left North Carolina to become a teacher in California. I would never again see that look of disappointment on someone's face and know that it was due to my actions. This is a valuable gift to be given, this knowledge. How fortunate I was to learn it at a young age. My brother Gayle, the wild and crazy one, gave me so much more than the hope chest. He helped give me *understanding*.

It was after I became a schoolteacher that I decided to pursue the goal of becoming a singer. I'm sure all those early memories made in my little hometown—along with some help from my husband—inspired me to write "The Happiest Girl in the Whole USA."

Gayle is retired now, but we still have a good laugh over the hope chest incident. Mount Airy hasn't changed much. O'Dell's Sandwich Shop still has the best hot dogs in America. And it seems like only yesterday that my friends and I were driving down Main Street, blowing our horns, with the boys pretending to be Elvis or James Dean, and the girls pretending to be their dates. Mount Airy gave me a good foundation for my dreams, the thread with which I was able to weave the tapestry of my life. And each time Christmas rolls around, I still get the urge to wrap up little gifts for all the visitors. But one thing is certain. If I ever see another big gift sitting under my tree, from my brother Gayle, I'm going to wait until he's there before I open it!

Tom T. Hall

"...a guitar and some Bill Monroe records..."

We had a lot of white Christmases in Kentucky. Our Christmas tree was one we cut from our farm. It would have been a joke to *buy* a Christmas tree in those days. My mother did the Christmas shopping. She always bought apples and oranges and hid them in the house. The smell of the fruit was one way we knew that Christmas was coming. We lived in the country in Kentucky. Oranges and apples were rare in winter. It was a nice smell.

We weren't poor when I was a child, but we lived on a strict budget, my father being a preacher. So I always envied the neat stuff the sinner kids got for Christmas.

I never wrote notes to Santa. Never believed in Santa as I remember it. He struck me as being as implausible as the many ghosts and goblins we heard about so often.

I remember one Christmas when my brother Quinton bought a guitar and some Bill Monroe records. The guitar was for me, and the records were shared by the whole family.

One Christmas I made a bow and arrow set for my younger brother. It was a real work of art. But he didn't like it so I kept it for myself.

For Christmas dinner we usually had roasted chicken with dressing. Plenty of sage in the dressing. It was the only time of year my mother used sage. It was a holiday aroma and she saved it for that.

I would like to see the commercialism taken out of Christmas. Jesus never made a big deal of his birthday; no reason we should humiliate poor people by demonstrating how much better off we are than they.

But I like the music.

Wade Hayes

BETHEL ACRES, OKLAHOMA

"...if you believe in Santa, then he's real..."

I'm from a little town on the flat, windy plains near Oklahoma City. Bethel Acres had a population of around twelve hundred while I was growing up, and it hasn't changed much since then. It's farm country out there, full of horses, cattle, wheat and alfalfa fields, blackjack trees and good people.

I was in grade school when I started to wonder about Santa Claus, and why nobody ever saw a guy flying around from house to house, dropping through chimneys and able to cover the whole world in one night. Finally, I asked my mom if he was real. "If you believe in him, then he's real," she said. I knew right then something was up.

Like many kids who loved music my best present was that first guitar, a Sigma Martin from my dad. Later that night my parents wondered about the wisdom of giving me that gift when they awakened to the first of many one-man, middle-of-the-night concerts blaring from my room. Of course, my dad's a musician, too. He knew what was coming.

I've never missed a Christmas in Oklahoma because for me, that's where Christmas is. I love the anticipation of driving home for the holidays, of getting closer and closer to my parents' front door. This year that drive was better than ever because, for the first time, I had enough money to buy my parents special gifts, instead of just whatever I could afford. I bought my dad a Fender amplifier, and Mom a pair of diamond earrings. Thanks to that Sigma Martin and those one-man, middle-of-the-night country concerts, I've been allowed the opportunity to experience *giving*. It was better to watch Mom and Dad open their gifts than to open one myself.

Loudilla Johnson

WILD HORSE, COLORADO

"...Mama made apple Santas..."

My parents grew up on poor dirt farms in Oklahoma. They were still in their twenties by the time we six children arrived, so money for Christmas presents was rare. But as we grew older, Daddy shared something with us that helped us better understand the holidays and gift-giving. It seems that he had been bitterly hurt as a child to learn that Santa didn't exist, that the adults whom he loved and trusted had "lied" to him. As he grew older and had his own family, he vowed to teach us children the truth, as best he knew it. Therefore, we may not have had money for gifts back in those childhood days, but we had something more special: the true meaning of this holy season. So Santa Claus didn't interfere with our celebrations. He only enhanced them.

We children grew up in Wild Horse, Colorado. Wild Horse is not the Colorado you see in travel posters. It's on the windswept eastern plains, where tumbleweeds roll and coyotes howl. Christmas at our house meant lots of nuts, candy, apples, oranges and, sometimes, bananas. Mama made popcorn balls and apple Santas with marshmallows for fur trim and figs for feet. No one we knew had a refrigerator, but if it was cold enough, Mama made Jell-O, putting it outside to set. If we had snow, she mixed it with cream and sugar for a unique blend of "ice cream." Food preparation went on for days and grandparents, uncles, aunts, and cousins gathered from miles around for the family Christmas dinner. Often, the relatives plowed through miles of mud, ice, and snow, over rutted and unpaved country roads just to gather. But they all made it. And we celebrated Christmas the way Daddy taught us it should be celebrated!

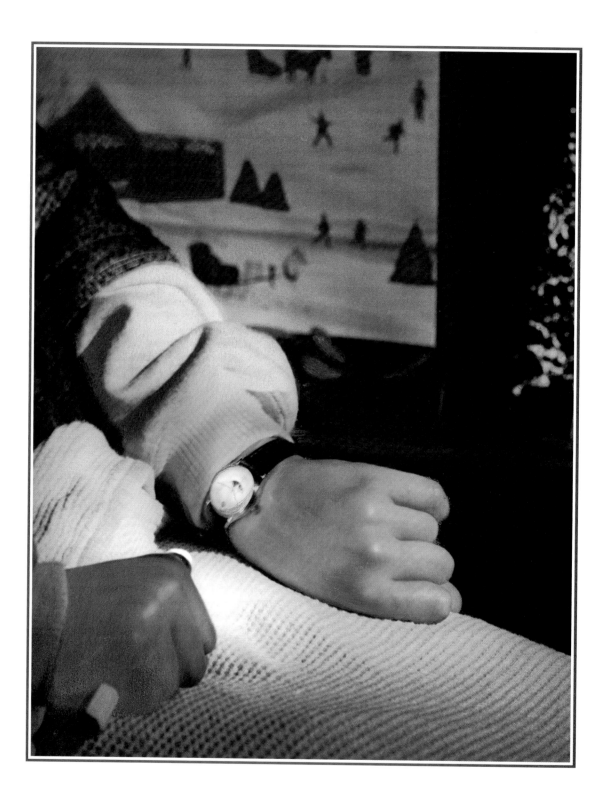

Hal Ketchum

GREENWICH, NEW YORK

"...we never waited until dawn..."

Sometimes when I reflect on the holidays I tell myself that I don't want to bring up sad times. Childhood was not all fun and games for me. My mother was ill with multiple sclerosis for all of my life, and on the surface of my memories lies that illness. When I think it through, though, under the veneer of illness and sadness is a truth. It's the truth about a woman who met illness with dignity—humor even—a very powerful woman who helped prepare food for the family's Christmas long after that first morning when my father had to help her to the kitchen. She was a woman who was in there swinging until the end.

Mother had her first bout with MS just after I was born in 1953. The illness comes and goes, and each attack leaves more permanent damage. Childbearing aggravates the condition, and after my birth, she went temporarily blind. No one knew what was wrong. Multiple sclerosis was not an easy thing to diagnose in those days, and some of her doctors thought it was psychosomatic. When my sister was born, Mother had another flare-up. As she got worse, doctors even advised that she be put in an institution to attempt to discover what mental processes were at work to make her believe she was ill. Mother was the kind of woman who wanted to know, too, so she went. Luckily, there was a medical professional who was interested in her case. Our family doctor began researching Mother's symptoms, and, finally, on the best and worst day our family had known, he discovered two things. Her illness was not psychosomatic. It was multiple sclerosis.

Multiple sclerosis is a slow conqueror. It takes people in their youth, just when life should be starting, just when they are beginning to enjoy growing up, or raising a family.

My parents had married in the post-World War II days, the Golden Age of Prosperity, when America believed in white picket fences and perfect Christmases where Mom gets up early to put the turkey in the oven. It took away that golden age for them, but the slow conqueror never quite beat them down.

We lived in Greenwich, New York, in the Adirondack Mountains, near the Vermont border. The mountains are actually a part of the Appalachians that begin up in Maine. It's an area defined by woods, lakes, and rivers. The next town is only eleven miles down the road, but it takes about a half hour to drive it because of the curves. It's one of the most beautiful spots I've ever seen, and it's still largely undiscovered. I hope I don't add to its "discoverability" by talking about it now.

Dad worked as a linotype operator and he eventually worked his way up from a small town newsman to the head of *USA Today*'s plant in Boston. He and my mother loved those mountains. They loved the world that was offered there. New York state is different from the stereotype we are used to. Just like people often think of the Appalachians as primarily southern, they think of New York state as primarily urban. We were anything but that. I lived a rural life, despite the fact that one of my greatest influences in Greenwich—my grandfather Ketchum—was a cosmopolitan individual. Even though Grandpa Curtis was a born and raised New Yorker, and a consummate reader who played the violin, our recreation centered around hunting and fishing, trap lines and hounds. I know it's not in vogue to say that now. On the other hand, I take a certain pride in knowing I can survive in the wilds, from the bounty of the land. I learned from many levels and many people.

The pioneer side of me extended to an entrepreneurial spirit, and Christmas was when the spirit best blossomed. My neighbor, Jimmy Fullerton, was my youthful partner in my enterprises. We mowed lawns in the summer and shoveled snow in the winter. The beauty of living in a four-season environment is that you always have a cash crop. Christmas was especially lucrative. In late November, in the Adirondack Mountains, you can find ground pines, long running vines of evergreen. It's not hard to take a coat hanger apart, curl it into a circle and wrap ground pine around it. We sold them as Christmas wreaths for three or four bucks apiece. It was a good business.

My mother encouraged our attempts to be business moguls, and she especially loved our Christmas wreaths. Our house was filled with them. It was a great old pre-Revolutionary farmhouse and filled at Christmas with music, as well as those wreaths. We were a very big and very musical family, of Irish and Scottish descent, players of banjos, fiddles, violins, and guitars. In addition to live music, we played our favorite records on our old phonograph. We especially loved the Christmas recordings of Nat King Cole, Andy Williams, Bing Crosby, the Andrews Sisters, and José Feliciano.

On Christmas Eve we always went to bed late, in anticipation of what the dawn would bring. But the truth is, we never waited until dawn. I, for one, started checking my watch with my little flashlight at around three in the morning. I'd look down at the numbers and see 3:04, 3:08, 3:15. I also checked the window. My parents had a rule that we couldn't get up until someone else in the neighborhood had turned their lights on. Fortunately, there were a few families on our street that we could count on, the families who had kids more spoiled than we were. These kids got up very, very early. A neighbor's light would twinkle and we'd shoot out of our rooms and down the stairs. Even then, the anticipation built. The next rule was that we could go only as far as the kitchen, where we could see, but not touch, what Santa had brought. Then Dad came down to the kitchen and had his first cup of coffee. Next, he helped Mother down, and only then did we open our gifts.

We did struggle through some holiday seasons. Anyone who has had a tragedy or an illness in their family knows what that means. But *short term* doesn't necessarily translate to less of a life. My mother knew her time was limited, so she made every minute with us count. And I had some great holidays in addition to the ones where we hurt. I had the good fortune to have a huge family around me—forty or fifty relatives at all holiday celebrations. My great-grandfather Ketchum sat around and told stories from his youth in Ireland, and I listened and loved the sense of history and tradition.

My mother not only listened, she participated. She was a great philosopher, so she used the years she had to impart every bit of family wisdom and family history she possibly could. She laid it on us. Christmas isn't a time to remember sadness. It's a time to remember the philosophers and strength-givers we have known. I remember one very well.

Chris LeDoux

KAYCEE, WYOMING

"...it took me five years to build that cabin..."

My father was in the military, so we lived all over the world while I was growing up. I was born in Biloxi, Mississippi, but we were only there for a few months, so I don't really have many memories of my birthplace. Traveling around as much as we did, I picked up things from all over the country that would later shape me into the person I am today. In Michigan, at my grandparents' farm, I learned a respect for the earth, and for the farmers who make their living from the soil. In Texas, I discovered my love of horses and rodeo. It was there that I began to dream, like a lot of other little boys, that I might grow up one day to be a champion rider. As I said, I saw a lot of the world traveling around with my dad. But it wasn't until I arrived in Wyoming and saw those vast open spaces—the temperature was ten below zero that day—that I knew I was finally home.

Because of Dad's military career, we were seldom able to celebrate Christmas with any relatives except our immediate family. One year we did make it to my grandparents' farm for the holidays. I remember being sure I could catch Santa in the act that night. I pretended I was going to bed, then came back into the living room and hid behind the couch to wait. Christmas morning they found me sound asleep and no wiser than I'd been on Christmas Eve.

Two childhood presents stand out in my memory, and these were certainly not the expensive kind like chemistry sets or erector sets. They were a hatchet and a rope. For a young boy like me—I already knew that the rodeo and cowboy life would be my niche in the world—those two gifts couldn't be beat.

When I proposed to my wife, Peggy, I told her the truth: I didn't have anything to offer her except one hundred and thirty dollars and a good horse in Amarillo. After we got married, we lived strictly from hand to mouth. We had little more than the hopes that I'd draw a good horse in the next rodeo. I finally managed to get a few acres near Kaycee, Wyoming, and Peggy and I moved into a tiny trailer on the property. Then I started hauling stone and logs down from the mountains. It took me five years to build that cabin, but I have seldom been prouder than the day it was finished. When I drove the last nail, I knew the cabin was all mine. I didn't owe the bank a penny. Peggy and I both remember the first year we were able to spend Christmas in what to us seemed like a palace. I cut down a huge tree, and we were truly home for the first time.

One Christmas that will always stand out in my memory was the Christmas of 1976. Throughout that holiday season I spent much of my time bandaged up and riding garbage cans. I should explain that I had received a lot of injuries the previous rodeo season, and most people figured I was washed up. All through that winter I holed up in Wyoming, finding better ways to wrap my injuries and rigging up garbage cans on ropes as modified bucking machines. Christmas—and the rest of that winter—may have been painful, but I learned that a dream can come true if you are willing to sweat some for it. When I arrived in Oklahoma City for the 1976 finals people were actually surprised that I even made the effort. In rodeo, folks bid on the contestants. They can win with them, just like in a horse race. I got "bought" for peanuts, but I didn't care. I just hoped I'd get a good, tough horse that wanted to throw me in the worst way. Those are the winners. I couldn't have drawn a better horse because Stormy Weather was known as one of the toughest on the circuit. He and I made the ride together and neither of us gave up, not until I'd won the 1976 World Championship in bareback bronc riding. I don't think a cowboy in the arena believed that I could come back that year, let alone win. But then, they didn't see me spending the winter on a bucking garbage can, either.

This year, Peggy and I and our five children finally moved into a big house we had built on our ranch. I didn't have to haul stone and logs this time, and we have many more acres than we had with the first cabin. We were so excited about having all the extra space that we put Christmas trees up all over the place. Each of the kids had their own tree in their room. And even though my kids seem to love music and sports more than ranching, I make sure they receive gifts they can use around here. They've all been given horses at various times, and this year I gave my oldest son a saddle. I had an ulterior motive with that present, however. It allowed me to get back my own saddle which he'd been using!

Kaycee, Wyoming, has a population of three hundred, and since that's the nearest town, it's no wonder that we're a very close-knit family. Actually, the town itself seems like one big family. I love it because it's got both its upstanding members and its black sheep members. Peggy's family lives nearby, so we always go to her house on Christmas Eve, open gifts and visit with all the in-laws and the cousins. Then we come back to our ranch that night and I read the Christmas story to the family. Then we put out eggnog and cookies for Santa, and have our private Christmas the next morning. My own kids usually haul themselves out of bed about four A.M., but they haven't had any better luck than I did at catching Santa in action. But he comes every year, just the same.

Patty Loveless

PIKEVILLE, KENTUCKY

"...we've been remembering that Christmas of 1966..."

There were a lot of children in my family, and my father was a coal miner back in Pikeville, Kentucky. So, some years, Christmas was really hard for him. You know, all daddies want to make sure their children get plenty of things from Santa Claus. One year Daddy didn't have much money at all. He was beside himself about what to do. Then, one of our neighbors gave him a good price on a puppy dog, so Daddy bought the dog for all of us. We kids didn't think anything about him not having a lot of money that year because that puppy was a bundle of love. It might be the best present any of us ever got!

My favorite Christmas memory of all concerns my oldest brother, Wayne, who was in the Army at the time. It was 1966, and Wayne had been sent overseas to Germany. We were quite certain that he would not be home for Christmas that year. We were such a close family that we could really feel it when one of us was missing.

My sister, Ruth, who lives in Columbus, Ohio, was driving in for the holiday with her own family. When she pulled up to the house, there was Wayne! It was such a surprise, and it was a Christmas wish come true for my mom and dad. It had been killing them that we might not all be together.

I've been talking to Wayne a lot lately, and we've both been remembering that Christmas of 1966, and how it felt that the family was able to celebrate together. It all came back to us as we talked, just like it had happened yesterday. It's hard to believe that the feeling is still so strong after all these years, but it is.

Barbara Mandrell

HOUSTON, TEXAS

"...we all sing Happy Birthday..."

I love Christmas. It's the season when business concerns fade away and I spend all my hours with family and friends. From the time I was a child, the Mandrells believed in doing things together during the holidays. My sisters, Louise and Irlene, and I decorated the tree, usually making ornaments with glue, glitter, construction paper, and popcorn. Since I was the oldest, and my mother didn't like to wrap presents, I wrapped everyone's gifts, including the ones to Louise and Irlene from Santa. I liked knowing something my little sisters didn't, and I kept it to myself. We opened presents on Christmas morning, and soon afterwards my sisters and I presented the holiday show for our mother, Mary, and our dad, Irby. Remember on our television show, where I was characterized as the bossy one? It's true. I'm the big, bossy sister. I wrote, produced, directed, and starred in all those childhood Christmas shows. I was watching a home movie of one of them years later, and noticed that since Irlene was so young that all she could do was sing a little, I made her skip around the tree while Louise and I acted out a little Christmas play. I obviously wanted action on the set at all times.

Another thing I always did as a yearly ritual was to separate all the gifts to see how many I had. I even volunteered to vacuum the rug around the tree, just to have the opportunity to rearrange and inventory the gifts. It is a habit I never lost. In 1969, a year after I got married, my husband, Ken Dudney, had to spend Christmas on his battleship, and I spent it at my parents' home. I was pregnant with our first child, but that didn't mean I was completely adult when it came to Christmas. As I had always done, I started rearranging and checking. To my surprise, I only had one tiny present, about the size of a lipstick! That present was so little our toy terrier, Dinky, thought it was one of his. As the days went by, I kept checking. Nothing. Christmas morning, same thing. Nobody said a word until several gifts had been opened, including my lipstick. My parents and sisters milked it for all it was worth. Then they wheeled out a doll buggy filled with my real presents, and laughed until tears were rolling down their faces. By the way, the gift I sent my husband to open on his ship was a pair of white boxer shorts that I'd decorated with red lace around the legs, and a big red "Merry Christmas" across the rear.

Since I was born on Christmas, we've separated the two events throughout my life. We have Christmas celebrating the birth of our Lord in the morning, then in the afternoon we have a wonderful tradition I got from Connie Smith, and just love. The children bake a birthday cake for baby Jesus. They've done that since they were tiny, no matter whether the refrigerator and the floor are covered in cake batter, or the sugar is spilled all over the table. Then we put one candle in the middle of the cake, and all sing Happy Birthday to Jesus. Later, we bring out my cake, and my birthday presents, which have been sitting on a table or on the book shelves, and I have my turn.

One of the most memorable times I've had was on the Christmas I turned sixteen. We were living in California by then, and our family band was entertaining at military bases. Dad played guitar, sang, and emceed. Mom played bass. Dad thought we should do a free concert for the guys stuck during the holiday season at Camp Pendleton. It was probably the toughest audience I've ever played, because those men wanted to be somewhere else. Finally my dad rolled the band to a halt, and said, "You men think you've got troubles. I've got this daughter named Barbara over here who just turned sixteen today. That makes me the father of an old maid!" That loosened them up and from then on it was a wonderful show.

As we Mandrell sisters got married and started our own families, our entire family's traditions changed. We now celebrate twice, beginning in mid-December, gathering the extended family whenever we can all get free time. We talk on the phone for hours discussing who is bringing what dish for Christmas dinner, and what time everybody will be arriving. We switch off houses. Sometimes it's at our parents' home, sometimes mine, sometimes Louise's or Irlene's. It's a time when the cousins can catch up with each other, and we can all relax and enjoy the company.

My husband and three children and I have been celebrating Christmas in Aspen, Colorado, for the past eighteen years. We tried starting that tradition a year earlier when the physician who delivered our children, Dr. Newt Lover, and his wife Janice, invited us to visit them on their skiing holiday. I think that was the only year in history that it didn't snow in Aspen, so we ended up going to Banff, in the Canadian Rockies. But we got to Aspen the following year, and we loved it so much we never stopped going.

When we bought a condo for those holidays in Aspen, we resisted buying a television at first. Our two older children, Matthew and Jaimie, were young at the time, and we started doing things as we had when I was a child, making decorations and playing games, instead of watching cartoons. There was no way to keep television out of our house for long, though. So now we set aside specific times for the traditions. We all still decorate and bake and play games when we aren't on the slopes. The community has made us feel right at home there, and this last year our youngest, Nathaniel, was even in the Christmas pageant.

Aspen is a magical place during the holiday season. Everyone is happy, and smiling, and laden with bright packages. The snow is heavy, the Christmas lights cause the whole town to sparkle, and it seems so much like the North Pole that you expect to see Santa and his eight reindeer soar over the housetops at any moment. But most importantly, at nine thousand feet above sea level, you feel very close to the reason we really celebrate this holiday: the birth of our Savior.

Martina McBride

SHARON, KANSAS

"...overwhelmed by the beauty of the night..."

Christmas meant a big family gathering in my hometown of Sharon, Kansas, not far from the Oklahoma border. My husband, John, is from there, too, so we always had the traditional holiday dinner with our families, sang carols, and exchanged gifts. But on December 22, 1994, here in Nashville, I gave birth to our first child, Delaney. We brought her home from the hospital on Christmas Eve and, for the first time, Christmas was a quiet affair with just the three of us. We put Delaney in her bassinet and opened our gifts when we felt like it, with no set schedule for the evening. We were overwhelmed by the peace and beauty of the night, and overjoyed with the new life that we had in our midst.

Delaney had arrived by Caesarian birth and I was not up to cooking a holiday dinner. So John and I decided to get our traditional turkey and dressing from the local Cracker Barrel restaurant. Shortly after he left to pick up the dinners, John phoned from the car. "I'm sorry," he said, "but nothing is open on Christmas Day but Waffle House." That was fine with me. "I'll have cheese grits and eggs, raisin toast, and hash browns," I told him. And that was our dinner the Christmas that Delaney came into our lives. Those Waffle House grits and eggs will always stand out as one of my favorite holiday memories.

Last year, as I was getting Delaney bundled up for her first Christmas in Kansas, I thought again of that joyous and peaceful holiday the previous year. As our daughter grows up I want her to understand how special her first Christmas Eve was. I want her to know about the immense love that filled our home that night.

Bob McDill

BEAUMONT, TEXAS

"...someone had assembled those bikes..."

Remember believing, *truly* believing, in Santa Claus? I was the last kid in my age group to admit that maybe he didn't exist. I even got into arguments on the playground with my friends. They'd laugh at me because I was still a believer. But wherever I went, I found myself defending the guy, as though I were a little Don Quixote, tilting at Christmas trees instead of windmills.

One memorable holiday cemented my faith in Santa Claus, the Christmas my dad was sick in the hospital. My brother and I got our first bicycles as gifts that year. There they were, under the tree on Christmas morning, all nicely put together. The boxes they had come in were out in the garage, so *someone* had assembled those heavy bikes. Mom wasn't known for being the mechanic of the family, but I asked her anyway. "I guess it was Santa," she said. This was all the proof I needed to allow me to hold onto my ideals for a while longer. And I presented it as ammunition to my friends, whenever they tried to tell me otherwise. It was my first excursion into deductive reasoning. *Major premise:* Someone had assembled the bicycles. *Minor premise:* Mom and Dad didn't do it. *Conclusion:* Santa lives!

It was only later that Mom finally told me the awful truth: My uncle had put the bikes together. It hurt, but I guess I was already exhibiting a love for fantasy and romance—as well as an early refusal to accept reality—that later followed me into songwriting. But middle age allows you to believe in a few magical things again. You become more spiritual as time passes. You know, I've just been sitting here thinking. Maybe it *wasn't* my uncle...

Dean Miller

SANTA FE, NEW MEXICO

"...a song he had written just for me..."

I was born Roger Dean Miller Jr., in Los Angeles, but Santa Fe, New Mexico, is my home. I lived there from the age of twelve, when I moved in permanently with my father, Roger Miller, and my stepmother, Mary. New Mexico is divided into two different types of country. Much of the southern part of the state is awe-inspiring desert, with a western-flavored history. In the north, you find equally awesome mountains and many laid-back artistic communities. One of the most wonderful things about life in that region is the deeply rooted multicultural aspect. It was settled by Spaniards hundreds of years ago, and even now there are areas where the spoken Spanish is almost identical to the Castilian Spanish of old Spain. It's the sort of place that inspires thought and creativity, the sort of place an immensely creative and free-spirited individual like Roger Miller would naturally love.

Almost anybody in Nashville who knew my father has a story about him, and they're almost always outrageously funny. One of the best involved the time Dad was stopped for speeding, and the officer said, "May I see your driver's license?" Dad answered, "I don't know, may I shoot your gun?" Another one had to do with one of his famous all-night shenanigans. He looked out his window to see a blazing sun coming up on the horizon. "Oh no," he said, "here comes God with his bright lights on!" I love them all, but my favorite Roger Miller story is a Christmas tale.

Dad loved having what he considered a Norman Rockwell kind of Christmas at our house in Santa Fe. He wanted everything decorated and beautiful during the holidays, but he didn't have much to do with making it happen. That job he delegated to Mary, and it didn't have anything to do with gender roles in the household. I think the reason he felt ill-equipped to "get in charge" of Christmas was that he had very few good childhood memories of Christmas himself. When Dad was barely a year old his father died. His mother could not provide for her three sons alone, so Dad was sent from his home in Texas to what the family called his uncle's "two mule cotton farm" in Oklahoma. It meant being separated from his brothers, and it only slightly improved his poverty-level existence.

My father picked cotton to earn enough money to buy his first guitar. That skill, combined with his way with words and his quick wit, eventually took him out of poverty. But poverty sometimes gets a hold on you, and never quite lets go. He loved the holidays for his children, but since he had no real experience with the rituals, he just handed the task to Mary. She made Christmas a wonderful time at the Miller household. She created a holiday straight out of the magazines, one that transformed our home into a magical world.

Since my father was sometimes uncomfortable with the seasonal details, it became even more important to me when he gave me the finest gift I've ever received. The year I was ten years old, Dad sat down and played a song he had written just for me, a Christmas song titled "Old Toy Trains." I cherished that song and listened to him singing it on tape hundreds of times while I was growing up. Much later I wrote a song for him, titled "Daddy's Shadow." I was too nervous to play it for him so I left the tape on his dresser.

In the autumn of 1992 my father died of cancer. He was only fifty-six years old, but the shadow he left is a long one, for he was a larger-than-life person. Having a parent like that could work for you or against you. You might feel overwhelmed by their success and just give up on your own dreams, or you might feel compelled to work harder to make them come true. I've worked harder and expected more of myself because of him. By the way, he loved "Daddy's Shadow," and I should never have worried that he wouldn't.

Over the years, and as is typical of a lot of people, I somehow forgot about what a special time Christmas is. Not that I didn't like it, I just didn't appreciate the spirit of the holiday as much. Then, when I was in my late teens, my radio alarm clock awakened me early Christmas morning. On the air was Roger Miller, singing "Old Toy Trains." Whatever spirit was lagging came soaring back over the airwaves, compliments of my father.

Old Toy Trains

BY ROGER MILLER

Chorus:

Old toy trains
Little toy tracks
Little toydrums coming from a sack
Carried by a man dressed in white and red
Little boy don't you think it's time you were in bed?

Verse 1:

Close your eyes
Listen to the skies
All is calm, all is well
Soon you'll hear
  Kris Kringle and
  the jingle bells
Bringin'

Repeat Chorus.

Mark Miller

DAYTON, OHIO

"...she pulled out the hippie outfit..."

For most of my childhood our family Christmas could have been scripted directly from *The Waltons*. My mother, my brother, Frank, and I lived with my grandfather on his farm, near Dayton, Ohio. Mom had three sisters who lived in the area, and counting all the kids I had twenty-one cousins. We were a very close family, but certainly not a rich one. My mother was raising us alone on a schoolteacher's salary and the farm was always a step away from being taken by the bank. Even so, we believed in getting Christmas presents for everyone. We weren't hip enough to think about drawing individual names, so I bought a gift for every cousin and every cousin bought one for me. With so little money available, the presents might be pencil sets or boxes of Life Savers, but they were wrapped and under the tree waiting for Christmas Eve. I loved shopping for everyone. It was second only to watching people open what I'd found them. We all felt that way. The excitement of seeing those packages start to mount up was such a high!

We had our big traditional dinner on Christmas Eve, then started the ritual of the madhouse gift exchange. With so many people involved we usually went on until after midnight. My best Christmas was when I was in the fourth grade and got my first electric guitar. I'd been hinting about it for months, and finally Mom said, "Mark, you've got one guitar and you can't even play that. I don't know what you want with another one." The old acoustic guitar that had been rattling around the farmhouse had four strings and no sound to speak of, and it was not one that I cared to play. But for the prize of an electric guitar, I'd do it. So I got a book on guitar chords and went to work. After a few weeks I could do a pretty passable job on "Your Cheatin' Heart." So I auditioned for Mom. She said, "Well, that was good." And that was it. I'd about given up on that guitar until the next Christmas Eve, when I pulled a suspicious-looking box out of the pile. It was just an old used electric guitar but it felt like a new Fender to me. I have no idea how she got the money together to pay for it, but she did.

One year Frank and I saved up to buy Mom clothes. It was the first year we'd been able to do anything more than just a small bottle of perfume, or a comb and brush set, so it was a major shopping event. Down to the store we went and we bought the coolest things we could find: a pair of bell-bottom cords and a tie-dye jacket. We didn't have a clue. Anybody who sees me today on stage knows my taste in clothes is, well, let's just say a little left of center. Mom's surprise that night was at the size of the box, which was three times bigger than any present we'd ever given her before. Then she opened it and pulled out the hippie outfit. She stared at those pants and that jacket for a minute. At first she just smiled. Then, she started to laugh. She thought we were playing a practical joke on her. When she realized that we were dead serious about the gift, she was horrified. Luckily, the cousins all thought the clothes were as cool as Frank and I did, so we managed to save a bit of face. I learned one thing that night, and that's if there's a generation gap, clothes may not be the best gift to give in order to close it!

While Frank and I were in junior high our idealistic existence took a nose-dive: The bank came and seized the farm. We were terrified by the whole experience, and you can still hear my resentment toward the harsh treatment of farmers in the songs I record today. A year or so later Mom found a teaching job in Apopka, Florida, so we packed up and moved south.

So much changed with that move. Some of the changes were little ones, the things you don't think about until years have passed. For one thing, the way I earned money for college was certainly different because of living in Florida. In Ohio I'd probably have done farm chores, such as driving a tractor or working with livestock. In Florida, I found a variety of jobs we'd never have envisioned back on the farm, including one stint as a water-skiing Pinocchio at Disney World!

Christmas remained a big event in our lives, even though all the cousins were back in Ohio and our family had grown very small. Mom and Frank and I eventually developed a Florida Christmas tradition: bowls of boiled shrimp. But for me, Christmas was still that farm, just outside Dayton, with what seemed like a million gifts under the tree.

Fate doesn't always take you where you think you want to be, but it can force you down a road that actually leads to the realization of a dream. The move to Florida falls into that category. It was while I was in college, at the University of Central Florida, that I met a lifelong friend and musical partner, Hobie Hubbard. I was totally into sports in school, and very serious about playing basketball. Of course, I knew the pros were not for me, being many inches shorter than those guys. And besides, I harbored a secret dream of becoming a songwriter. That's when I heard about an English major named Hobie and learned that he was as serious about his writing—short stories at the time—as I was about basketball. It seemed like a perfect match, so I looked him up at the pizza parlor where he worked. I must admit that I was wondering all the time what he'd think about some jock who was wanting to be a songwriter. Well, he took me seriously, and we started working toward coming to Nashville with our songs.

Years later, after we'd founded Sawyer Brown and started making a little money, I began gathering people back around me. Frank joined the organization in management, and several of the cousins signed on in various capacities. My mom moved to Nashville. It wasn't until several years ago, when Frank and I bought a farm, that we realized we were recreating our childhoods. Today, we again celebrate Christmas in that old *Walton's* style. The cousins all come to Mom's house and we buy presents for everybody. The bigger the pile under the tree, the more I like it. One thing, though. We'll buy Mom anything but clothes!

Ronnie Milsap

ROBBINSVILLE, NORTH CAROLINA

"...four hundred miles to my mountain home..."

Until the age of five I lived in the North Carolina Smoky Mountains. We lived in semi-isolation, with cabins located miles apart. Socializing usually occurred at church meetings or at the little general store in the valley, where several old men whittled the day away and mountain folks gathered to exchange news. My parents divorced soon after I was born, so I was raised by my grandparents. The outside world considered us impoverished hillbillies, but because we had never known anything else, we didn't feel poor. Likewise, I was born blind, but having never known sight, I didn't feel pitiful.

Because I couldn't see a Christmas tree or read a Christmas book, my holidays existed in *sound* and *smell* and *touch*. Christmas meant something different to me than it does to sighted people. It meant that the cabin would fill up with the voices of neighbors, folks coming to bring freshly baked goods; that my grandparents and I would make more trips down to the general store; that the smell of the little pine tree my grandfather had cut would fill the house; and it meant the anticipation of receiving a sweet-smelling orange, or a rough, hard English walnut. Christmas meant *family* and *friends* and *fellowship*.

When I was five years old my grandparents made a difficult decision about my life, but one made for the good of my future. They sent me away to Raleigh, North Carolina, to the Governor Morehead School for the Blind. Back then blind children weren't mainstreamed, so if we had any hopes of making it in the work world, we had to go somewhere for an education. I lived and studied at Morehead until I graduated from high school. My fellow students became like a second family to me. It was there that I experienced the camaraderie of new friends and the excitement of caroling parties and Christmas concerts. Each year the Morehead School caroled all around Raleigh, ending up for hot chocolate and Christmas cookies at one of the instructor's homes. It gave us a warm feeling, knowing we could give something back to the city and its people.

Because it's such an obvious art form for a blind child to pursue, we were a very music-oriented school. I studied violin and later became enamored of the piano. It was my love of keyboards that allowed me to work my entire life. Many of us blind students got jobs as piano tuners for the Raleigh school system. As a young teen, I saved my earnings and bought presents for my family and school chums. My roommate, Jay Spell, and I were ham radio nuts. Each holiday we made sure we saved a couple of dollars so that we could get each other some small present related to our hobby. Sometimes we gave each other a set of radio tubes and other times things like a Morse Code Keyer.

If we earned more than usual we might splurge and indulge our other great love: records. The school only allowed us to play classical music, but Jay and I loved rhythm and blues and rock 'n' roll. So we might ask some trusted person to take us to town to buy a Fats Domino or Little Richard record. We also found a way to circumvent the ban on rock 'n' roll. Both of us played piano so we would sign up for a practice room together. There we perfected the art of playing rock music until we heard someone coming down the hall. Then, within one or two notes, we'd switch into Bach. I guess the school not only taught us how to survive as blind people, it taught us to be innovative as well.

We students stayed at Morehead each year until December 23rd, then went home until January 2nd. My grandparents had no car so I rode a bus the four hundred miles from Raleigh to my mountain home. A school official would take me to the station and alert the driver that one of the Morehead kids was traveling with him. The driver would then take care to guide me into the station when we had rest stops, show me where the snack stand was, and help me with my bag when we finally arrived. It's funny when I think about it now. I wouldn't have allowed my son to ride a bus alone for fifty miles when he was six or seven, and he's sighted. But times were different in the 1950s. We had no choice.

My years at Morehead were invaluable. I eventually won a full scholarship to study law at Emory University. But music was my first love, so I bailed out of a career in law and started playing piano for J. J. Cale. My old friend and roommate Jay Spell went on to perform with people like Jimmy Buffett. He now plays keyboards with me in my show. When we're onstage together, it seems like only yesterday that we were young teenagers, switching from Fats to Bach in a couple of notes.

Christmas took on a new meaning for me when I married my wife, Joyce, in 1965. I must admit that when Joyce brought a blind musician home her parents were understandably concerned that she'd end up a caretaker. They hadn't seen that little boy taking a bus for four hundred miles alone, or sneaking rock 'n' roll music into a classical school. Joyce assured them that I wasn't helpless. We've been married over thirty years now, and whatever success I have I lay at her feet. I may not be helpless, but I'd be much less without her.

Joyce always made the holiday season special, and after our son, Todd, was born, it became even more so. When Todd was just a baby I started a tradition of sitting at the piano on Christmas Eve, my small son on my lap, playing Christmas carols in front of the tree. I'd listen as the elaborate decorations were described to me. What a thrill to know that I was able to give gifts I'd never dreamed possible. I began insisting that every Christmas be videotaped. Even if I couldn't see the replays, I could picture the beauty of it in my mind. As Todd grew older I loved plotting and planning what gifts to give him. One year it was a go-cart and another it was an antique Model-T, things he wanted with all his heart. Thankfully, my son ended up unspoiled!

Like back in those North Carolina Smoky Mountains, Joyce and I put a great deal of importance on inviting friends over. At our house Christmas morning is for the immediate family, and Christmas Eve is for our extended family, which includes friends and neighbors. We exchange gifts and people bring favorite foods, just like folks did all those years ago. The best Christmas of all was in 1994, when Todd and his wife, Ruth, brought their daughter, Kye Leigh, to our home for her first Christmas. As I sat at the piano with my granddaughter in my lap, I felt that same satisfaction I did as a four-year-old, sitting on the cabin floor, listening to my grandparents talk with the other mountain people about their blessings. What a wonderful world we live in, that this could all happen in a lifetime!

Jimmy C. Newman

MAMOU, LOUISIANA

"...that little car probably cost twenty-five cents..."

In 1682, the French explorer La Salle came down the Mississippi River and named the territory he found there "Louisiana," in honor of King Louis XIV. It wasn't until much later that we acquired the nickname of "The Pelican State," thanks to the pelicans that were living in great numbers along the gulf coast. My own ancestors were Acadians, expelled from Nova Scotia because they refused to swear allegiance to the King of England. So, around 1760, they left Canada and headed down the same river as La Salle. It was in the bayous of Louisiana that they found a new life and a new culture for themselves. We're known as Cajuns now, an anglicized version of the word "Acadians."

It was Louisiana's strategic position—we lie astride the mighty Mississippi, and we sit atop the Gulf of Mexico—that brought about the Louisiana Purchase of 1803. But we have modern boasts, too. Those fuel tanks you see on the space shuttle are made in our state, and so were the C-5 boosters used in the Apollo moon landing. Modern advances mean other changes, too. Unfortunately, those pelicans that gave our state its nickname are now almost extinct. And it looks like the old-time Cajun trappers who still cruise the bayous in hand-carved pirogues, the way their ancestors did, may not be far behind the pelicans.

There was no town where I grew up. We lived ten miles from Mamou, in Evangeline Parish. (We're the only state in the country with parishes instead of counties.) This is the piney woods part of Louisiana, right where the bayous end and the creeks start. So I was raised between bayous and creeks. That terrain isn't as muddy as the bayou. The pine belt runs through there, all the way from East Texas to South Carolina.

81

We spoke French, of course, a patois, but we celebrated Christmas the way everyone else did. I'm sure that I won't be alone if I say that times were hard back in those days, because for some of us they were. My father, who was an invalid, ran a country store. My folks were always busy taking care of the store. And my mother had her garden to tend to, not to mention her children. In those early years we did put up a Christmas tree. I suppose it was my big brother who actually cut the tree and brought it home. We were in pine country there and so I still remember that pine odor throughout the house at Christmastime. If I remember correctly, Mother decorated the tree, mostly with popcorn garlands.

We children never gave gifts to each other, or even to our parents. It was unheard of for a child to have any money for presents. Some Christmases we got apples and oranges, and that was quite a novelty. The one gift we each received would be put in our Christmas stockings, which were hung on the fireplace chimney. In those days, our fireplace and chimney were made out of mud, a red clay. When Cajuns gather to help build whatever needs building, we call it a *coup de main,* which literally translates to "stroke of hand." In military terms, it means a surprise attack, but to us Cajuns it's our own version of a good old-fashioned *barn-raising.* And that's how our mud chimney was constructed, with the help of friends and neighbors. First, they made the formation of the chimney out of pine slats and then covered it with a mixture of red clay and pine needles. The needles were added to get the clay to stick. In later years we graduated to a brick chimney, but in those early days our stockings hung from the mud one. Despite hard times, I must say that it was a wonderful thing to wake up on Christmas morning and know that our stockings were hanging from the chimney with some little toy inside.

Three special gifts from those childhood years stand out in my mind. I received the first—a little ceramic cowboy—when I was about four years old. All my life I've been a great admirer of cowboys and the Old West, and it may very well have begun with that first present. The next memorable gift was a cap pistol, complete with a holster. But the one Christmas present that has stayed foremost in my mind all these years probably didn't cost more than twenty-five cents. It was a little light green car with battery-powered headlights. The headlights were really little flashlight bulbs. The only batteries we had back then were one size, a regular flashlight battery, so it had to fit under the hood of the car. There was a switch to turn the lights on and off. Gosh, I thought that was something! My friends and I made roads in the yard and we had a big time. I was only about six years old but I have never forgotten my first car.

We never had a white Christmas in Evangeline Parish. I do remember snow falling one year, and me tracking rabbits on that freshly fallen white, but that's my only memory of a Louisiana snowfall. We had Cajun foods on Christmas, gumbos, rice and gravy, chicken fixed with different sauces. I don't ever remember eating *fried* chicken as a child. Because turkeys couldn't survive in our area for some reason, they weren't raised there. So we never had turkey as a holiday dinner. The table fare was typically Cajun-style.

I have another special Christmas memory from those early years. This one was back in 1946, when I was just starting out as a performer, ten years before I joined the Grand Ole Opry. My band and I were playing a Cajun Christmas Eve party in Eunice, Louisiana. Our host invited us to stay overnight. Now, Cajuns are famous for dancing and singing and eating and having a big time. And that's what we all did, that Christmas of 1946. The whole band went home with our host and spent the night as his guests. The next morning, we woke up to a fine Christmas gumbo.

These days Mae and I live on our farm in Rutherford County, Tennessee. Our address is Jimmy C. Newman Road, and we got 670 acres to spread out on. But we celebrate Christmas in Lafayette, Louisiana, with our son, Gary, his wife, Sharon, and our only grandchild, Natalie, who is ten years old. Again, the dinner is usually Cajun-style. We do have turkey these days as part of the fare, but it's smoked and spiced in the Cajun tradition, along with Cajun-style rice dressing. Gary and Sharon usually have some Cajun ornaments on their tree, little alligators and crawfish. Being together with family is the most important part of any holiday, but that first Christmas with Natalie in our lives is one that will always stand out for Mae and me. Then, this past year, on December 23rd, the city of Mamou presented me with the key to the city. On top of that, I was finally inducted into the world renowned "Fred's Lounge Wall of Fame." Christmas can't get much better than that!

Stella Parton

"...we were allowed to touch the button jar..."

I grew up in the enchanted forest of the East Tennessee Smoky Mountains. My family are mountain folks. We are proud, independent, and resourceful. Being of Scottish, Irish, and English descent, we've had lots of traditions handed down to us from another place and time. Yet, surviving in the Appalachian Mountains taught several generations of my relatives to be creative in their own special way.

Being on a limited budget Mom was truly the "mother of invention." And decorating our Christmas tree was no exception. Each December, Daddy always managed to pick the most perfect cedar tree that grew on our farm. This sweet-smelling cedar was placed in a large bucket of sand and gravel, and then wrapped with one of Mom's new, handmade quilt tops. These pieces of my mother's art would later be sewn into warm quilts during the cold winter months that arrived after the holidays. Since Mom was very "crafty" with her hands, she always cut a perfect star out of cardboard and wrapped it gently in aluminum foil. (We called it "tenfol" back in the mountains.) It was the first ornament to adorn our tree. Then Daddy would eventually get around to mentioning what a perfect cedar he'd managed to find that year, maybe the prettiest one ever. Mom always agreed with him. "And I do believe that's the best star I've made up 'til now," she'd add. Daddy and all of us children thought so too. And there were eleven of us kids, so how could we be wrong?

When it came to decorating, Mom gave each of us wonderful jobs so that everyone would feel special by the ornaments we created for our family tree. This was the only time of year that we were allowed to touch the treasured button jar. The center of attention, it was placed in the middle of the living room floor. We children were each given a needle and thread and, slowly, those colorful buttons turned into beautiful strands to twist around the tree. Then, my brothers would dip cones and sycamore balls into a sticky flour mixture to give them the appearance of snow. They were then laid out to dry on a paper bag or, as we call it, a "paper poke." Some of the children strung berries and popcorn into garlands. Daddy and the boys whittled thread spools into tiny toys with their pocket knives. The smaller children colored pictures brought home by the older children, half-finished, so that the little ones would have a chance to color as well. The next morning these decorations were all placed on the tree by the child who had proudly made each one. Even the leftover aluminum foil from Mom's star was rolled into little silver balls and strategically placed to create a shiny effect. Our tree remained a "work in progress" as the holiday unfolded. As Christmas cards arrived in the mailbox from family and friends they were also hung on the tree. If a family member was lucky enough to find some holly, or mistletoe, it was brought home and put over the door, or in the windows.

My daddy was a tobacco farmer in those days and money was in short supply. If there was a bad tobacco crop there would be no presents. I think the most wonderful Christmas gift I ever received in my childhood was a little dresser set. It was clear blue plastic and sold for twenty cents. But I treasured that gift from my parents. I can still remember the tiny comb and brush, the handheld mirror that seemed so magical.

Even as a child, I knew things before they happened. Around Christmastime I'd see an image of Mr. Fletcher coming along the road in his ancient green truck. The Methodist Church always sent things during Christmas for mountain children in East Tennessee, and Mr. Fletcher delivered the goods. I thought Santa Claus drove an old green pickup truck until I was twelve years old. My sisters were convinced I was a gypsy because I could guess the day Mr. Fletcher would come. "It's getting serious, girls," I'd tell them. "You better fix your hair and your makeup. I believe I see Mr. Fletcher coming now. His truck is loaded with toys, apples, oranges, candy, and clothes that are good as new." Then my sisters would threaten to snitch on me. "We're going to tell Mama," they'd say, "and she'll tell Grandpa Jake. He'll cast the devil out of you, because telling the future is of the devil."

We also got our share of rich tourists, driving past in their fine cars. I could never understand why they found us so fascinating, but they drove up our hollow to say, "Look, dear, at the little hillbilly children." I felt sorry for their kids. Poor rich kids. I used to wish they could have the magic we had in our Tennessee mountain home at Christmastime.

Lots of years have passed since those early Christmases, but I still maintain some family traditions. For instance, my tree is a "work in progress" all through the holidays. I just move things around, maybe add a bow from a present someone has given me. Sometimes, I find colorful beads in my jewelry drawer that look perfect on the tree. This year, I was adding things to my tree on the very day I took it down!

My son, Tim, and I have our own rituals. He puts up the star, or angel, or whatever we choose for the top of the tree. We started this tradition when he was a year old, and I had to hold him up so that he could help me. Nothing else is put on the tree until I snap a photo of him smiling at me. When I was a child back in the Smokies, my family sang most of the traditional carols as we decorated the tree. Tim, on the other hand, has always liked Elvis's Christmas album. This was an album I had when Tim was small, so it means something special to him. This past holiday all my Christmas decorations were in storage, so I rushed out to a record store to purchase the Elvis Christmas CD. I half expected the sales-girl to chuckle at the idea of Elvis music at Christmastime but, to my surprise, she said, "Oh, I wish I had grown up with a Christmas tradition like that. Your son is so lucky!"

My mother and daddy are now in their seventies. This past Christmas the Partons converged for what we call "The Family Christmas Gathering." Mom made the aluminum star again, and Daddy helped the grandchildren and great-grandchildren pick the perfect cedar tree on our farm. Some things never change. And through the season most people are nicer and kinder to each other. Maybe we should practice the Christmas spirit all year long. Like the Parton family tree, maybe our lives are "works in progress," always needing a little touching up. After all, fellowship shouldn't be like that jar of buttons, something we touch once a year. Instead, it should be given freely, a gift that will shine all through our lifetimes, just like that old "tenfol" star. Friends and family are the real treasures. And, oh yes, let's not forget Elvis's Christmas CD!

Gretchen Peters

PELHAM MANOR, NEW YORK

"...we made the pipe into an ornament..."

Christmas is about rituals. Over the years some of the rituals have changed, either by necessity or by design, but the essence of Christmas lives in the little things we do year after year. When I was a small girl, we lived in a picture-postcard town called Pelham Manor, just outside of New York City. It was my father who started a lot of the traditions that we practiced, almost slavishly, each year. Weeks before Christmas we would start making ornaments. In our house there was always a competitive spirit, and points were given for originality. I remember a bejewelled Indian elephant that my grandmother made (it still hangs on my tree every year) and a tiny China doll head complete with long pigtails that was made by my father. There were trips to F A O Schwartz, the famous, awe-inspiring toy store in Manhattan, and to Rockefeller Center to skate and gawk at the huge Christmas tree. There is nothing like Christmas in New York.

On Christmas Eve we were sent to bed, and my father, William Peters, who is a writer, would begin composing the banner which he hung across the top of the stairs each year. The banner was designed not only to amuse us children, but to keep us from going downstairs where the presents were until everyone was awake Christmas morning. Every year the banner had a different theme. I remember one year it was a space-age message: *Keep Out! Dangerous! Strontium Santas! Atomic Air Guns! X-Ray Xylophones! Nuclear-Powered Puppy Dogs! Titanium Tinsel!* In the morning we'd line up at the top of the stairs and go down one at a time, oldest first, which meant I was always last. Years later I was told my parents wanted us to do this so that they could get a good look at our faces when we saw what Santa Claus had brought. And, of course, they could also catch us if, in our haste, we tumbled down the last few steps.

My father was also a stickler for wrapping gifts so that you could never guess what was inside. If you were getting a hockey stick, it would be wrapped to look like an umbrella. If it was something tiny, it would be wrapped in several boxes, each one larger than the next. We were expected to guess the contents before we tore open the paper, and he delighted in fooling us. There was always one unwrapped gift, something large and wonderful, waiting at the bottom of the stairs. But all of the other gifts had to wait until after we ate a formal, sit-down breakfast in the dining room. It was excruciating, but it made Christmas morning last a lot longer.

When my parents divorced things changed. It was a difficult time for everyone, and I think it was especially hard for my parents to figure out how to make Christmas feel like Christmas again. My father remarried and moved to Manhattan. Instead of having him home for the holidays my sister and I visited him at his and my stepmother's apartment. My stepmother, who is Jewish, went out of her way to celebrate Christmas with us. She went shopping for beautiful ornaments to hang on her "tree," which wasn't a Douglas fir but a very large tropical plant she had in her living room. It made for a very exotic, if somewhat irregular, Christmas tree. But her enthusiasm and sense of humor prevailed.

A few years later my mother, Ann, and I moved to Boulder, Colorado, and began a new and very different life. There was less money and less family. We went from being a household of seven, to just two or three members. But there was certainly no less fun. We instigated new rituals. Since the traditional family Christmas was no longer possible, we began adopting Christmas "orphans." These were friends and acquaintances who either couldn't or wouldn't go home for the holidays and would otherwise be alone. The fact is, we almost always had someone living at our house in Boulder. Sometimes it was a University of Colorado student who needed a room, or a friend of a friend who just happened to be passing through Boulder. My mother worked at the Colorado Mountain Club and constantly met itinerant climbers en route from the Himalayas or some exotic place. Often there was a whole houseful of people, a pot of chili on the stove, maybe a slide show of someone's trip to China, and a whole lot of good music bouncing off the walls.

When I was still a teenager, Mother and I spent a Christmas Eve with friends at a club in Boulder, listening to one of my favorite bands. I had begun playing guitar by this time, and at Christmas I always brushed up on my favorite carols and insisted that everybody sing. I think I held on to the more traditional holiday rituals, like singing carols and baking cookies, as a way of holding on to the memories of my childhood. Boulder in the 1970s was wild, freewheeling and fun, but I wanted order in my life, especially at Christmas.

One of my best Christmas memories started out as a disaster. It was one of our first Nashville Christmases, and besides myself, my husband, Green, and our daughter, Caitlin, my mother and my best friend were staying with us in our small apartment. Several of us had the flu. There had been a terrible cold snap and—it was Christmas Eve at precisely midnight—a pipe burst in the wall and water began gushing out. Complete chaos ensued. Before we got the water turned off, the hallway was flooded, carpet soaked, and wallboard destroyed. We were all tired, sick, and struggling to see humor in this situation. We called the maintenance man, David, who had been up all night dealing with broken water pipes and power outages. Yet, he came cheerfully to fix the pipe at three A.M. Christmas morning. We served coffee cake and coffee, and David presented us with the two-inch-long length of copper pipe which had disrupted our long winter's nap. We made the pipe into an ornament, engraved with the year of the disaster. It remains one of my favorite decorations.

I still hang on to the rituals of Christmas. These days, I don't always have time to make ornaments, so I try to buy them while I'm traveling. I bought a beautiful tin star in Mexico, some little voodoo charms in New Orleans, and a tiny gold replica of F A O Schwartz in New York. One year Green and I took Caitlin to New York for Christmas and showed her Rockefeller Plaza, Central Park, Fifth Avenue, all my old childhood haunts. But the essence of Christmas to me is people. Every year we have several "orphans" who come and spend the holiday with us. Together, we plan a beautiful Christmas Eve dinner, and then we have what amounts to a huge slumber party with friends and family sleeping wherever there's available space. I've had both traditional and nonconformist Christmases, and they're all wonderful, as long as you've got people you love around you.

Jeanne Pruett

"...the gift of dignity..."

My father and mother, Kirby and Estelle Bowman, were cotton mill workers. In Alabama there used to be a great many Avondale textile mills where a lot of the local people worked. Mamma and Daddy were full-time farmers as well. But Daddy only grew cotton for a year; you couldn't eat it or put it in a fruit jar, so he didn't raise it anymore. There were ten of us children in the family, with two or three years separating us in age. While we always had a lot of food to eat there were very few frills in our lives. Being a big family with a meager income meant that mother sewed our clothes from Purina feed sacks, the cotton sacks that feed for cows was packaged in. Mamma never had a pattern to go by. She'd get her measurements by holding the material up to our bodies, and then she'd sit down at the sewing machine and whip up a dress or a shirt.

Back in those days it was left up to us kids to get a Christmas tree and decorate it. Sometimes we'd cut down a pine tree—there weren't many cedars in our part of the country—and then we'd color paper strips and glue them together to make chains to put on the tree. We never had any store-bought decorations that I can ever remember. Once the paper chains were on the tree we'd add red berries, or anything that we could find with some color to it. A couple folks who were regular visitors to our home happened to be cigar smokers. They smoked cigars that came wrapped in little gold-colored bands. So we used those bands for decorations. We used anything that had some *shine*.

The best Christmas I remember could have been my worst, had I let it. I've never told this story before. Even my children will be surprised to read it. Earlier, I mentioned Purina feed sacks. When you say "feed sacks" most people think of rough, heavy burlap. But these sacks were made from a printed cotton fabric of excellent quality, like the material you'd buy in a store. I think Purina was the first to package feed in this manner. It may have been an ingenious marketing idea: If a farmer bought several sacks of feed packaged in similar fabric there would be enough material to make a garment of some kind.

The Christmas I was thirteen my gift was a new dress which Mamma had made from feed sacks. The print was of small yellow daisies spread out across a cream-colored background. It had a gathered skirt, round collar, and puff sleeves with little bands. The sashes on each side tied into a bow at the back. It wasn't an elegant pattern, but I sure didn't think it looked like it had once been a feed sack. And so, that first morning after Christmas vacation, I climbed onto the school bus feeling very stylish in my new dress. Determined that it wouldn't get wrinkled, I found an empty seat and spread the skirt out carefully. Then I sat back, certain that I was the envy of every girl.

As was customary with a country school bus, it stopped at neighboring farms along the way to pick up schoolchildren. At one of these farms a boy got on board. I'll never forget what happened next. I looked up and saw that he was wearing a shirt made from the same print as my dress: small yellow daisies on a cream-colored background. Then I thought I would surely die, because a girl stood up at the front of the bus and said, very loudly, "Jeanne is saving you a seat at the back. You'll fit right in." I knew this girl. She was always doing something to attract attention to herself. I don't know if she ever realized how much she hurt our feelings. When I think back on it, she was probably as poor as a church mouse, just like the rest of us.

The boy never said anything. But our eyes met as he moved toward my seat. We were both thinking the same thing: "Everybody knows we're wearing feed sacks." He sat down next to me. When I looked over, I saw tears running down his face. They were running down my face, too. But we never spoke. Poor kids don't have to talk about being poor.

How could this be my best Christmas ever? I'll tell you how. This was the day I decided that I would never let what other people say hurt my feelings. You might consider it a Christmas present that I gave *myself* that year. I had all day to think about what happened, and the truth was quite simple. My *mother* had made that Christmas dress, and she worked long hard hours. She wasn't just a farm wife and mother to ten children, she was a working woman, too. If she wasn't at her mill job, she was in the kitchen, or the garden. If she wasn't sewing or cooking, she was shelling peas, or breaking beans, or milking cows and getting the milk cooled down for children to drink. My *mother* had made that dress. So, when I got home from school, I thanked her for it. I told her how pretty everyone thought it was, but I never, ever, told her the truth about how much I had hurt. And from that day forward the feed sack dress became my favorite. Wherever I went, I wore it proudly. I would give anything in the world if that little dress were in my possession today.

Mamma and Daddy have passed away. I guess that when the holiday season rolls around, we all find ourselves thinking of the loved ones we've lost. My mother was seventy-five years old when she died. Daddy was seventy-seven. If they were still alive, Mamma would be ninety-four, and Daddy would be ninety-nine. This is amazing to me. This is how time can get away, without your realizing it. In my mind, I still see them vibrant as ever, sitting under the peach trees, peeling peaches, canning vegetables, and putting them away for winter. In my memory they will always be hardworking country people, doing the best they could with every day that God sent them.

I've received many expensive Christmas gifts in the years since I've left Pell City, Alabama. Often, when I'm in my dressing room at the Grand Ole Opry, getting ready for a show, I think of that day on the school bus, and the feed sack dress with its little puff sleeves. It doesn't matter how many elegant designer dresses, or how many fabulous stage outfits I might wear, when I take them off I can still put myself right back in that seat, on that old school bus. And I realize that, but for the grace of God, I could still be there. And then I think of that boy, standing there in the shirt his own mother had sewn for him, most likely as a Christmas gift. I wonder whatever happened to him. Maybe he's a doctor now. Or a lawyer. Or a farmer, like his daddy would've been. Over the years I've tried to remember his name, but it's lost to me. Wherever he is, whatever profession he chose, I hope that he's been happy, and that life has treated him well. And I hope that when he got off the school bus that day, he got off carrying what I did: the gift of dignity.

Collin Raye

DEQUEEN, ARKANSAS

"...you never had to look for a guitar..."

So many members of my family are musicians that the holiday season was always filled with music. My mother, Lois, and brother, Scott, both performed. At our house, you never had to look far for a guitar and someone who was ready to sing Christmas songs.

During the holidays I try to spend as much time as possible with my children, Jacob and Britanny. They're my priority, my most valuable gift in this life. I want to know they'll be taken care of, that they'll be secure. But I also want them to value the right things. For so many years before I started making money from my music, Christmas was tough. It's hard to want to give your children gifts and simply not be able to afford them. You walk past store windows and it seems like everything you see is something you want your child to open on Christmas morning.

In 1991 my financial status took a turn for the better, when my first number one song, "Love, Me," started up the charts. The song meant a lot to me personally because it's about love that lasts a lifetime and beyond, the kind of love we all want. It also meant that my children would have the Christmas I'd always hoped to give them. I rushed out to all the stores where I'd previously only window-shopped, and I bought the kids present after present. Then I stopped and thought about what I was doing. I thought about Christmas, and values, and what I wanted my children to learn. I gave them what I'd bought up to that point, but I decided that I wouldn't go overboard. After all, the meaning of the holiday season is peace and love, and those two things don't come gift-wrapped.

Johnny Russell

SUNFLOWER COUNTY, MISSISSIPPI

"...wishing hard for that jacket..."

I was born in a sharecropper's shack, in Sunflower County, Mississippi, during a very heavy snowfall. In those days, Daddy was sharecropping with a doctor by the name of Dr. Weeks. When it came time for me to be born somebody went and got Dr. Weeks. This was in late January, and they tell me that the snow was three or four feet deep that winter, which is rare for Mississippi cotton country. But Dr. Weeks made it over to our little shack and he delivered me. I've also been told that my mother could turn the worst-looking place into the most comfortable home imaginable. And that's what she had done to the share-cropper's shack. She took flour sacks and sewed them into curtains to hang in the windows, and she made that place a home where her family could live comfortably.

It was sometime after I was born that we moved into the town of Moorhead, Mississippi. At that time, Moorhead had about two thousand people and a single traffic light. It's in Moorhead that the Southern crosses the Dog. Almost everybody in the South knows that poem, about the Southern Railroad crossing the Yellow Dog Railroad. This is where I remember my first Christmases taking place.

My sister, June, was a lot older than I was, and so she knew the truth about Santa Claus. I remember one Christmas morning, when I was about four years old, June said to me, "I heard Santa Claus." She was really playing it up. So I said, "Yeah, I heard him too, up on the roof." This surprised her. She looked at me and said, "You did *not*." She was old enough to know the truth, but not old enough to carry off the deception.

I was about seven or eight years old the year I was told there was no Santa Claus. It was the Christmas that I really wanted a maroon and gray school jacket, from the little grammar school I attended in Moorhead. So there I was: really wishing hard for that jacket, and then comes the news that Santa didn't even exist. But my parents had a big surprise for me. They had bought me the jacket and stored it at a neighbor's house. My sister took me over there to get it. But that was when I knew that gifts were from my parents, and not Santa.

About three years ago I celebrated Christmas in a way that my family and I will always remember. I was with my daughter and her family, and my son and his family, for the first time in a long time. My daughter, my daughter-in-law, and I stopped by the post office just before Christmas to pick up my mail. Songwriters are paid by royalty checks for the songs they've had recorded, and that day there just happened to be a royalty check waiting in my box. I hardly ever open those checks when they come. My sister, Patsy, who is my secretary, always opens my mail. But that day something made me tear open the envelope. I looked at the check inside and said, "Oh, my God." Then my daughter took it and looked at it. "I guess the grandkids get anything they want, don't they?" she asked. It was the biggest royalty check I'd gotten in years for "Act Naturally," a song I wrote that was a hit for both Buck Owens and the Beatles. This check was from the initial sales of all the CDs which had included the song. I mean, it was a *big* check. So we went shopping. "We're gonna get the kids whatever they ask for," I said. And that's what we did. My grandson wanted a Dallas Cowboys jacket. We had a hard time finding one—the Cowboys charge a lot more for their jackets than Moorhead Grammar School did—but we eventually tracked one down. My family isn't materialistic, so we didn't spend a lot of money. My daughter and daughter-in-law found little things they wanted, inexpensive earrings, perfume, and items like that. We didn't spend a lot of money, but we had a lot of fun.

This past year I'd been performing in Pigeon Forge, over in the Tennessee Smoky Mountains, for most of the summer and fall. When Christmas rolled around I was in the process of getting resituated in Nashville. My daughter and her family were scheduled to arrive from Texas for the holidays, and my son and his wife, who live in Nashville, were coming over. With my housekeeper's help I managed to get the house ready for my family.

But I didn't buy a Christmas gift for anyone, and I didn't even put up a Christmas tree. My daughter arrived on December 23rd. The day before Christmas we got up and went to one of my favorite Nashville restaurants for lunch. Then we bought a Christmas tree and, later that night, we decorated it. That was a very enjoyable evening with my family. On Christmas day I gave my grandkids money instead of presents, and they loved it. They went shopping on the 26th, hit all those big sales, and bought whatever they wanted. I wouldn't care to do that every year, but that was a fun holiday to remember.

I still remember one Christmas very well. It was years ago, shortly after I'd come to Nashville. The holiday season was rolling around and the financial situation was pretty grim. This was when I'd finally decided that I wanted to be an artist as well as a songwriter. I'd just begun to make records and travel on the road. I had one show date in the entire month of December. This meant that I would make $125 that month, and no more. Then, out of the blue, an old friend of mine from Texas phoned me up. His name is Carl Johnson and he owns the Rio Palm Isle in Longview, Texas. Carl called and said, "How's Christmas?" I told him it was going to be okay. Then he asked, "What are y'all getting for the kids?" I told him I didn't know just yet, but we'd get something for them. So then he said, "You got any money?" I told him I didn't, but that we'd be okay. "You know," Carl said, "it doesn't bother me too much how you and your wife might be doing. But it bothers me about those kids." Two days later I got a check in the mail for a thousand dollars. And Carl never let me pay it back. I worked a lot of dates for him down at the Rio Palm Isle— everybody from Sinatra to Elvis to Bob Wills has played there—but he never docked me that thousand dollars. As a matter of fact, I just remembered that I owe Carl Johnson some money that he probably *would* like back.

Christmas isn't my favorite time of year. There's just too much pressure that comes with it. That's why this past holiday was kind of nice. Everyone had plenty of gifts to open because my son and daughter brought gifts with them. Then, on Christmas morning, we cooked a big breakfast, which we do every year. My mother, who is now eighty-three, was there with us. This is what the holiday should be about anyway, the opportunity to sit back with your loved ones and just spend time together.

Daryle Singletary

WHIGHAM, GEORGIA

"...you need to go down to the corral..."

I grew up on a little farm, near a small town called Whigham, Georgia, population about six hundred. Some of my earliest and best memories involve singing songs with my great-grandmother. Although Christmas was a big event at our home, I personally don't put much value on receiving gifts. For me, the holiday is more about giving and receiving *love*. One gift and one Christmas, however, stand out in my mind from all others. I was about fifteen years old, and I wanted a horse more than anything. A family acquaintance had been allowing me to ride his horse, so I mentioned to my parents how much I'd love to have a horse of my own. But I certainly wasn't expecting one.

That holiday season was one of the coldest we could remember around Whigham. The town lies way down south in the state, only about fifteen miles from the Florida line, so we weren't used to cold Georgia winters. To keep the water from freezing in the pipes out by the corral, we had to let it run all night. That Christmas morning we got up early. My dad led the conversation around to the fact that it seemed to be warming up some outside. "You need to go down to the corral and turn the water off," he said, his expression not telling me that something special was up. So I put on my coat and walked on down to the corral. There stood the horse, the most beautiful sight I'd ever seen! I found out later that Dad had picked him up in the middle of the night, as a Christmas morning surprise. That horse was without a doubt my best Christmas present ever.

Connie Smith

"...all the kids laughed at the purple star..."

My most vivid Christmas memories are the ones I've shared with my own children, and not the ones of my childhood. Funny, but I can tell you that the very first time I ever came to Nashville was March 28, 1964, when I sang at Ernest Tubb's Record Shop! *That* I remember, but I don't have clear memories of the early holidays.

I was born in Elkhart, Indiana, but when I was five months old my family moved to Forest Hill, West Virginia. We lived in a camp on the banks of the Greenbrier River. That's the first home I recall. Forest Hill is just south of the Allegheny Mountains, about twenty miles west of where the Appalachian Trail twists and winds its way south. West Virginia is a sight to behold. Back in the late 1700s Thomas Jefferson stood at the junction of the Potomac and Shenandoah rivers, in the eastern panhandle, and looked out at the breathtaking scene before him. "It's worth a voyage across the Atlantic," he wrote in his journal.

When the Greenbrier River rose enough to spill over its banks, we had to pack up and move into town. When the water was high, Mama sat up at night and kept a close watch on the river, in case of flooding. A stick had been driven into the ground in the front yard, as a water marker. I remember many times of waking in the middle of the night to see Mama sitting in her chair, reading a Zane Grey book, keeping a quiet vigil while her children slept. At intervals, she'd put her book down and go outside to check the water around that stick. When the level had risen dangerously high, she'd come in and wake us all up. We'd get dressed and go out into the darkness with just a flashlight to guide us. Sometimes that water would be up around the porch steps so high that we'd have to jump to get across it. Then we'd go up to the roadside and catch the Zelco bus—that was the name of the bus line—and we'd go to my Aunt Ora's house in town until the water receded.

When I was about nine years old we moved to southern Ohio, where most of my growing up took place. We moved around so much in those days that I went to eight different schools. So, I don't think of one town as being home. In Ohio, I lived near the Big Bend Tunnel and the very railroad on which the legendary John Henry was said to have swung a hammer. We used to play in those tunnels—unbeknownst to Mother—until we saw a train coming at us. Then we'd fly like the wind, racing out ahead of it. It was always fun to watch the train go by and wave at the engineer. On those days when he didn't wave back, we threw rocks at the train!

Being in southern Ohio we always had a white Christmas. We cut our own tree and decorated it with popcorn that we kids had strung. There were fourteen children in my family, and we were very poor. We knew that our gifts were from Mama and Daddy, and not Santa Claus. So I don't remember ever believing in Santa. One of the greatest gifts we got at Christmas time was oranges. This was something we would never be able to buy at any other time of year. So, to have oranges and nuts and hard candy, well, that was special. Mama made a lot of our clothes out of flour sacks. Most of the presents we got were homemade, and something that we really needed. For instance, I didn't have a real doll when I was growing up. I remember one year I got a little doll, about six inches high, with a ceramic head and a cloth body. It wasn't much, but when my step-sister broke it, I cried for a long time. I know she must have felt terrible about that.

When I was a child we always had a lot of good food for our Christmas dinner because my mother was a great cook. But one holiday dinner that stands out in my mind, again, had to do with my own family. I have five children, Darren, Kerry, Julie, Jeanne, and Jodi. Darren is a missionary in Oslo, Norway, so that's where my grandchildren live. Three years ago I took the four other kids and we flew to Norway to spend Christmas with Darren, Sigrid, and the grandbabies, Rueben, Kaia, and Marina. In Norway they have a tradition which involves bowls of rice. One of the bowls has a nut in it. The person who finds that nut gets a special gift. That was a memorable Christmas for all of us.

One of the most fun times we had at Christmas was the year we decorated our tree with fake snow. We were tossing it on the tree and before long a "snow fight" had broken out. There we were, throwing fistfuls of that fake snow at each other. One of my young ones, Jeanne, got down on the floor and started making snow angels in the fake snow, right there on the carpet in our front room!

There was always a friendly competition when it came to actually decorating the tree, too. One year a friend of ours made little decorations, one for each of us; it was a constant squabble to see whose decoration would hang from the front of the tree. Every time one of us came into the room, we'd move our own decoration out to the front of the tree, and move the one already there to the back! This has gone on for years now.

We had many decorations that the kids made in school and, therefore, were special to us. Those were the ones we put on the tree until they simply fell apart with age. But one of the most talked-about decorations in our family was made by my son, Kerry. This one stands out because the incident was so traumatic to him. One year, when Kerry was little, his class at school made ornaments from dough, which they then painted. Kerry's was a small star and he painted it purple. All the kids laughed at his purple star. He came home from school crying and I had to console him as best I could. Then, one of the points on his star broke off, and we glued it back on. Today, even though it's crumbling all apart—Kerry is now twenty-seven years old—we still put his purple star on the tree. And someone is always moving it to the back and replacing it with their own decoration.

After I left home and had my own family, I began the ritual of making a birthday cake every Christmas. I've been doing this since the kids were little. On the top of the cake I write the words: *Happy Birthday, Jesus.* I've always wanted my children to know the real reason we're celebrating Christmas.

Three years ago my mother passed away. She was a precious woman. I'll always treasure that early memory of her, sitting in that chair with her Zane Grey book, looking out for us children while we slept. I've still got her old Singer sewing machine, the very one she made our clothes on. My mother represents another tradition I have learned to celebrate and appreciate each year: the importance of a kind and loving soul.

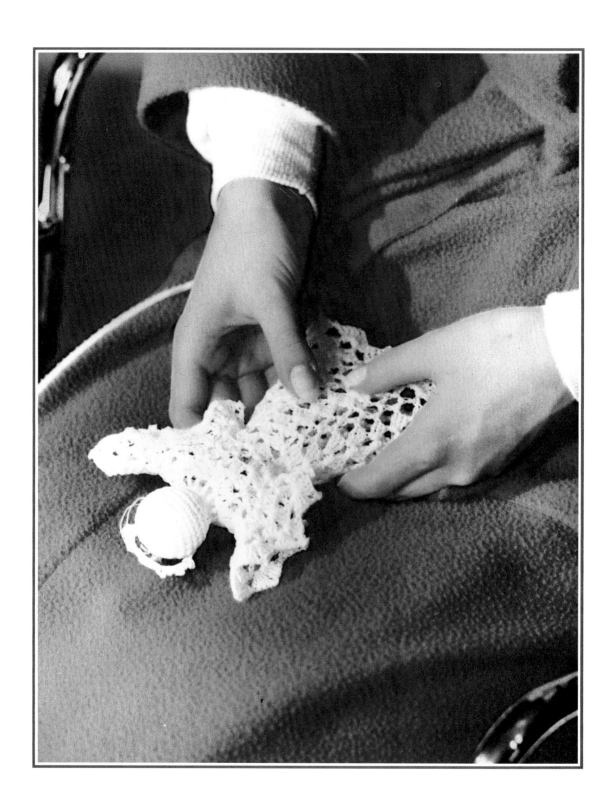

Pam Tillis

NASHVILLE, TENNESSEE

"...when I opened my eyes, I saw Mom and Dad..."

Christmas at the Tillis house when I was a child wasn't what you might think. We played Christmas records and things like that, but it was a time when my father, Mel Tillis, got to take a break from music and come in off the road after playing some two hundred and fifty dates a year. So while my brothers and sisters and I did all the regular musical things, like caroling with our church group and singing in the church Christmas pageants, we didn't make Christmas a "music" event at home.

For one thing, Dad needed the time off to be with his family and to rest up from being an entertainer. And he needed that time to just be a father. So it was a very normal kind of Christmas for the family, and not a star-studded holiday where Roger Miller and Porter Waggoner stopped by to swap gifts and sing songs with us—like you see in a country music television special! It was just our immediate family sharing the holidays with friends and neighbors who had nothing to do with show business. One year, Dad had a pal of his dress up like Santa Claus for my friends and me, and we believed he was absolutely the real one.

Because I grew up in Tennessee, where we get more ice than snow, a white Christmas was almost unheard of. So we always hoped for it, wished for it, and if we got it, we were more than thankful! I could probably count those white Nashville Christmases on one hand, but the times we had them were unbelievable.

When I think of my father's Christmas traditions both then and now, I think more of food than music, because what he loves to do during the holidays is cook. It's true. Mel

Tillis is a wonderful cook, and at no time during the year does he do it more than at Christmas. He makes pies and cookies, and everything he bakes is wonderful. Dad makes a terrific Christmas gumbo, too, so our holiday meals aren't always traditional. We stretch the season out as long as possible and make many, many meals during the celebration.

We all liked to make things at Christmas, whether it was food or decorations. We strung popcorn for the tree, and created ornaments and other decorations for the house. I love to sew, so many of the things I made were created at the sewing machine. My mother, Doris, loves angels and she still makes new angel ornaments every year. We love to design ornaments from lace and paper—angels, snowflakes, that kind of thing. Mother has two trees every year. One is the traditional Christmas tree, and the other has almost an Easter motif, a rebirth of love and hope. She fills that second tree with lambs, and we are always on the lookout each year for new ones to add to it.

Christmas isn't always a fairy-tale season, when everything is a perfect time, with snow falling and carolers outside your door. I think many of us have had Christmases that fell short of our expectations. Sometimes it's because you've lost someone during the previous year, and other times it's because you're having family difficulties. My very best Christmas—the time I learned more about what the season truly means—started out to be one of those unpleasant holidays.

When I was a teenager my wonderful, family-oriented Christmases appeared to be over, threatened forever by my parents' divorce. All those happy holiday seasons with two loving parents crumbled before my eyes. The fun times watching my father cook, and my mother make lace angels, rolled to an abrupt halt. I simply couldn't believe what was happening to us. Suddenly, Christmas became a cruel joke. On Christmas Eve, that very first year of their separation, I went out with some friends and we started drinking. It was a bad answer to a bad situation, and it got even worse when someone suggested we go driving around. But I went along with it, and jumped into the backseat of the car. I was unhappy, and feeling very lonely on that Christmas Eve. The last thing I remember before waking up in the hospital on Christmas morning was the sound of screeching brakes.

As I began to regain consciousness, I felt a terrible dread. Not only had I been out drinking, but I'd been involved in a car accident. I was afraid my parents would never forgive me. But when I opened my eyes, I saw Mom and Dad standing over me. On their faces I saw nothing but unconditional love and parental concern. When I tried to apologize, to somehow explain, they just shook their heads and let me know that all they cared about was the fact that I was going to be all right. I told them I felt like the worst daughter in the world. But they assured me that I wasn't a bad kid. Just a *confused* kid. I looked up at them from beneath my bandages, and I knew in that moment that nothing I could do would make them not love me. I also knew that even though they were divorcing, they were still a team when it came to me. The peace that filled my heart that Christmas morning came from the total forgiveness my parents offered.

I also know that all of us need to try and solve our problems in positive ways, not self-destructive ones. Life presents many problems for a lot of folks, and especially teenagers. Those tender years are when it's most tempting to combine drinking and automobiles. Teens aren't allowed in bars, and their parents probably don't allow them to drink at home. So when difficulties present themselves, they may try and find the solution while driving around with a beer in their hands. My own experience—what could have been the worst Christmas my parents ever had to endure, losing a child—reinforces the truth about that method of problem solving. It just doesn't work, and I'm thankful to be alive to say it.

I know life isn't perfect. It doesn't always happen the way you think it should. Life isn't a television special. I also went through a divorce, and I tried very hard to make my young son understand that divorce doesn't mean a child is less loved. The most important thing a child of divorce can know is that he or she did not cause the problems in their parents' marriage. During those years following my divorce, my son and I always decorated a little tree at our house, and then we went to both my mother's and father's home for Christmas festivities. Dad still cooks. Mother still makes lovely ornaments. Circumstances may change, but the traditions survive. And in recent years my mother has come to Dad's house to celebrate. That same forgiveness and understanding that I felt all those years ago lives today between my parents. And while I know Christmas isn't always out of the storybooks, it can certainly have a happy ending!

Aaron Tippin

PENSACOLA, FLORIDA

"...thousands of soldiers so far from home..."

When I was in my early twenties I didn't have time for "that Christmas thing." All the holiday season meant to me was buying the presents I had to, having Christmas, and being done with it. Because the day didn't have as much meaning to me I began a tradition that I still keep: I give Christmas to someone else. I worked manual labor all my life until I started singing, so I'd volunteer to stay on the job and work overtime so that the other guys could be with their families.

During the Gulf War, I traveled to Saudi Arabia with Bob Hope to entertain the troops at Christmas. When I explained my upcoming absence during the holidays to my daughter, Charla, I told her we were both giving up our time together so that a lot of soldiers could have a more enjoyable holiday. That trip with Bob Hope gave me back the spirit of Christmas. Seeing those thousands of soldiers so far from home, and so appreciative of us sharing our own Christmas with them, filled me with an unbelievable sense of the true meaning of the day.

Now Christmas has come to be my favorite time of the year. Part of that is because of Charla. I finally remarried this year and my wife, Thea, and I celebrated our first Christmas as a married couple in a new log home in Smithville, Tennessee. We went out on the property and chopped down a little, almost scraggly tree, just like Charlie Brown's. Then we decorated it with the Christmas ornaments my fans had sent us over the past year. Now I have decorating fever. Remember Chevy Chase in *Christmas Vacation*? Next year, that's gonna be me, the guy whose house lights up half the state.

Tanya Tucker

WILLCOX, ARIZONA

"...it must be Santa coming early..."

The town I was born in is Seminole, Texas, but when I was still a baby, we moved to Willcox, Arizona, where I spent most of my youth. My dad heard he could find work in Willcox drilling water wells, and since he was always looking for a way to better our financial situation, we packed up and moved. Dad had been working in the Texas oil fields long enough to know he wasn't going to make much money as a roughneck, no matter how many backbreaking hours he put in. By saving up for his own drilling equipment, he thought he might eventually be able to work for himself, instead of for other people.

Willcox was originally a railroad town, one of the many built after the rails finally got that far west. The town is in Cochise County, in the Sulphur Springs Valley, near the Chiricahua and Dos Cabezas mountain ranges. Cochise waged war against the U.S. Army for years throughout those plains and mountains. Although he eventually lost the battle, in one way he won the war: The county was named in his honor. Long after the Indian wars were over, Willcox remained a wild and woolly place. The old timers love to tell stories about when Warren Earp, Wyatt's brother, was murdered there, and when Big Nose Kate, Doc Holliday's companion, retired to the area. I believe my love of everything that smacks of the Old West began right there in the Sulphur Springs Valley. It was also there that I have my earliest memories of Christmas.

The Tuckers always celebrated the holiday season twice when I was growing up. The family exchanged presents on Christmas Eve, and then we got presents from Santa on

Christmas morning. One year—I guess I was about eight—we stayed up very late on Christmas Eve. My brother, Don, and my sister, LaCosta, were there. All of a sudden there was a big thump on the ceiling of the trailer. My dad said, "It must be Santa coming early!" We ran outside, and there up on top of the trailer sat a play-by-number organ. I couldn't believe it! I kept looking up at the sky to see if I could catch Santa flying away. Later, I realized that Don had slipped out for a while, but at the time I was too excited to think about it. I played that little organ a lot, but never considered it more than a toy. So, unfortunately, I never really learned to play keyboards or piano. Right now my six-year-old daughter, Presley, is taking piano lessons. As soon as she learns, she's going to teach me.

I'll always remember how my parents paid for my Christmas present one year. We had a tape recorder that Mom and Dad figured I needed to make demo tapes. This was when we were still trying to interest someone in my music. The tape recorder was in the shop, and it was going to cost quite a bit to fix it. So Dad sold it to the dealer for parts and bought me a bicycle and a puppy. I'll never forget seeing that puppy in a little doll's bed under the tree!

Our Christmas dinners have always been very traditional—ham and turkey and dressing, peas, corn, green beans, mashed potatoes. A couple of years ago I told my mom that I wanted to try something different, and hired a caterer to handle a holiday dinner. It was wonderful, and the food couldn't have been better. But it wasn't the same. It was a little like the year we loaded a Christmas tree, presents, the whole works, onto my bus and had our Christmas in Lake Tahoe. It was fun, but it wasn't home and I missed the tradition.

Some of my best Christmas memories are of sitting down to turkey and dressing. If you ask my son Grayson what he loves most at Christmas, he'll say it's the drumstick before he even mention presents! Presley would probably say, "Christmas cookies." These days, when I pay for the food we eat on holidays, I wonder how we could afford the meal—let alone the Christmas presents—back when I was very little. Of course, I didn't know then how poor we were, but looking back now I don't know how Mom and Dad made it through the Christmas season. Remember the great Merle Haggard song, "If We Make It Through December"? The words of that song are very real to some folks, and hit close to home. Yet I never felt anything but loved and provided for in my childhood years.

I guess having had so little back then makes me aware of people who struggle through the holiday seasons. I really try to give something back during Christmas. I often hear people say that the holidays are depressing. The older I get, the more I understand why. But this is because the meaning of the holiday gets outstripped by commercialism. Children see all these things on television and they can't understand why they can't have at least one of those toys. I've tried very hard to keep the spirit and meaning of the season in front of my kids. I read the story of baby Jesus to them, and spend a lot of time explaining to them that the season is about giving, as well as receiving. That's not to say they lack for presents. But they learn how much fun it is when they *give* a gift.

My staff and I try to deliver presents and food each year. One time we loaded presents and Santa Claus himself on Loretta Lynn's flatbed truck. Then we drove around singing carols and delivering Christmas dinners and gifts to quite a few families. Usually we take one of my tour buses, because the temperature fell below zero that year and the flatbed got real chilly!

One year we did it a different way, and I was so sorry we did. We thought more families could be included if we made it into an event. We collected a lot of names, and a list of which kids needed things like shoes and coats, in addition to toys. Then we invited everyone to a Christmas party at a local firehouse. It all seemed fine while we sang carols. But when one of the firemen started calling out names of families and they came forward to collect their dinners and presents, I got a sick feeling in my stomach. In my heart, I knew it was somehow degrading, like standing in a soup line or something. Maybe we can't help as many families when we visit each home privately, but there's more dignity to it.

I guess my story is proof of how fast your situation in life can change. We went from being poor to having money quickly when my career took off. It was so strange to be thirteen years old and suddenly be the *Santa* of the family. But I don't think there's anything I like more than giving presents, so it was a wonderful kind of strange. Family is the most important thing you have. You can lose money, and you can lose material things, but if you lose your family, you've lost it all.

Steve Wariner

NOBLESVILLE, INDIANA

"...we sneaked down the stairs..."

My grade school buddies were always trying to convince me to change my birthday from December 25th to June or July. They assured me I'd get more presents that way, and I'm sure they were right. My parents had five kids and Christmas was always a hard financial time. But I didn't mind the fact that I might get a little less. And being a Christmas baby just meant that the season was all the more highly anticipated.

My parents moved from Kentucky to Noblesville, Indiana, before I was born. My dad worked at the local foundry in Noblesville, making car parts. At that time, about half of the town's population was made of transplants from Tennessee and Kentucky who had come to look for work at the foundry, or in the mills. These days, Indianapolis has grown almost completely around the town of Noblesville, but back then it was a thirty-minute drive to the big city, and an adventure every time we went.

We lived right next to the railroad tracks, and even though the trains caused our house to rattle at night, it was still exciting to hear them whistling past. Every afternoon that we could manage it, we'd gather near the tracks and wait for the caboose to finally go by. We could usually count on the trainman to be out there, throwing candy off the back for us to find. These days, we live in times fraught with danger. Imagine children being given candy by a stranger these days. I hate to see some of the small-town, old-time ways disappearing from our culture, but they are.

My holiday traditions have changed since I married and had my own children. When

I was a kid, my family loved draping a big aluminum garland around the Christmas tree. We had one of those lights that revolve, making the whole tree change colors. I can still hear it creaking as it turned. You don't see those mechanisms anymore. Putting the angel on the tree was a big deal. This was done only after we kids had finished throwing great handfuls of icicles onto the tree, the floor, and each other. Then, Dad would carefully place the angel on the tree's top, and we'd all stand back and congratulate ourselves on a job well done.

I remember one year, when I was about six, one of my older brothers told me that he knew a big secret. "Santa is really Mom and Dad," he said. I didn't believe it for a minute, so he said he'd prove it to me. That night, we waited upstairs until long after we should have been asleep. Finally, we heard noises downstairs. "That's them," he whispered. "Let's go!" So we sneaked down the stairs and sure enough, there my parents were, putting all of Santa's packages under the tree. I thought, "No, it can't be." We sneaked back up the stairs and when we got back in our beds I whispered, "I wish you wouldn't have told me." It was true. I would've liked to have held onto Santa another year or so.

The most memorable Christmas I ever had was in the mid-1960s, when I got one of the first G.I. Joe dolls. This was before they were known as "action figures." My dad had been a navy man, and I loved to hear him tell stories about his military life. So, my mother chose a G.I. Joe in a navy costume, complete with the blue bell-bottoms and a duffel bag. I got a football that year, too, making it about perfect as far as I could tell. It might seem odd, since I'm known as a guitar player, but I never asked for a guitar while I was a kid. My dad was a picker, and since he already had a guitar, I figured that would be the kind of expense we didn't need and couldn't afford. We just shared.

I loved going back to Indiana for Christmas, and taking presents to all my family. One year, soon after I moved to Nashville, it must have been 1974 or 1975, I loaded my Camaro with presents and took off. There was no way I should have tried to drive home that year because we were having one of the worst storms in ages. It took all day and half the night, driving on the only lane left open. And to top it all off, I could barely see a thing, thanks to the snow pelting my windshield and the pile of the presents in the back seat that

blocked my rear view. When I finally pulled into the drive, I thought, "Well, I shouldn't have done it, not with all those snowflakes coming down, but I'm glad that I did!"

Now, my wife and boys and I always celebrate Christmas in the morning, and my birthday that night. My wife Caryn takes pains to see that the two are completely separate. On Christmas morning, the boys get up early and come wake us. Then we go downstairs, and while the boys and I look through the packages and separate the gifts, Caryn gets the coffee and orange juice ready. I always videotape the exchange of gifts, and I love getting out tapes from years past, to watch the boys grinning and showing off their new presents. Then, we have our big traditional Christmas dinner in the formal dining room, which is one of the two or three times a year we use it.

A few years ago I had the surprise of my life on Christmas morning. I'd been driving an old rattling pickup truck around Nashville for years, and Caryn had been trying to get me to trade it in. I didn't see any reason to because it was running good and it was paid for. I counted on driving that truck until it simply gave out. Several months before Christmas, Caryn brought up the subject and even spread some brochures out before me on the kitchen table. I did see a truck I liked a lot, a black GM. So I said I'd think about it, come the next spring. Without me knowing, Caryn went out and bought that very truck. She got it a week before Christmas and hid it in our neighbor's garage. It sat there, with a great big bow on it, just waiting. The family got up, and did the usual Christmas morning things. As Caryn was making the coffee she said, "Steve, I forgot a present out in my van. Would you go out and get it for me?" So, I put my coat on and headed out the door. Meanwhile, Caryn rushed out the back door and around the side of the house so that she could film me discovering the new truck. I was stunned. It's very unusual for us to give large items like that at Christmas, but Caryn said she just *had* to do it. I told her it was wonderful, and it was. Now, I'm really going to drive this one until it finally quits on me.

Bryan White

LAWTON, OKLAHOMA

"...Grandma White's Is Christmas Headquarters..."

We've always celebrated Christmas at Grandma and Grandpa White's house in Oklahoma City. Even after my parents divorced and Christmas tended to be split between two families, Grandma White's was considered Christmas Headquarters. Thankfully—and this is the best Christmas present ever—my parents have remained friends. Mom even sometimes comes to the Whites' to celebrate with us.

When my brother Daniel and I were little we couldn't wait to get to Grandma White's early so that we could help put up the outside lights. For many years Christmas meant spending time with aunts, uncles, and cousins. I don't know how it started, but the family slowly drifted apart. We'd get together, open presents, and then pack up the cars and head back to our respective homes. Maybe the fast-paced lives we were leading made us forget why the holiday is so important. Whatever the cause, Christmas had become a habit.

Then in 1990 something wonderful happened. People sat around visiting a long time after the gifts were opened. Everyone seemed to be in mellow moods. No one was anxious to leave. People talked in little groups here and there throughout the house and, finally, we found ourselves all congregated in the kitchen. There must have been more than fifteen people in there. Someone suggested we join hands and offer individual thanks. Then someone else suggested we share feelings about ourselves as a family. What quickly emerged was the fact that we all were beginning to understand how a family can drift apart, and why that mustn't happen. I'm not exaggerating when I say that there wasn't a dry eye in that kitchen. I don't think we'll ever be complacent about Christmas again.

Recipes

Bill Anderson

CHRISTMAS-CRANBERRY BREAD

This is such an easy Christmas bread to prepare, and it makes a wonderful gift during the holidays.

1	cup fresh cranberries, chopped	3/4	cup sugar
2	cups sifted flour	3	teaspoons baking powder
		1/2	cup walnuts

Combine above ingredients in large mixing bowl.

2	eggs	1	teaspoon vanilla
1/4	cup melted butter	1	cup milk

Preheat oven to 350° F.

Beat the eggs slightly and mix with melted butter, vanilla, and milk. Make a depression in the center of the cranberry mixture and pour in the egg mixture. Stir until dry ingredients are moist. Pour into greased 9 x 5 bread pan. Bake for 55 minutes.

SERVES 4-6

John Berry

FRESH CRANBERRY SALAD

This salad, which we serve every year during the Christmas season, looks very festive on the holiday table, especially when garnished with sour cream and pineapple chunks.

2 *cups water*
3/4 *cup sugar*
3 *cups (12 oz.) cranberries*
1 *6-oz. package orange-flavored gelatin*
1 *8 1/4-oz. can crushed pineapple, with syrup*
1/2 *cup chopped celery or walnuts*
Salad greens

In 2-quart saucepan, heat water and sugar to boiling. Boil 1 minute. Add cranberries. Heat to boiling, and boil 5 minutes. Stir in gelatin until dissolved. Stir in pineapple (with syrup) and celery or walnuts. Pour into 6-cup mold or 8 individual molds. Refrigerate until firm, at least 6 hours. Remove from mold and place on bed of salad greens.

SERVES 8

Suzy Bogguss

Squash & Apple Casserole

Here's one of my favorite holiday side dishes. You can easily substitute sweet potatoes for squash. This recipe is easy as pie to make and tastes as good, too!

4 cups sweet squash (like butternut), peeled, cut into medium pieces

2 large tart apples, peeled and sliced

$1^1/_2$ tablespoons butter

$^1/_4$ cup orange juice

$^1/_2$ teaspoon cinnamon

$^1/_4$ teaspoon ground cloves

Salt and pepper to taste

Preheat oven to 350° F.

Put the squash and apples in a baking dish and dot with butter. Pour in orange juice and sprinkle with spices. Bake for 50 minutes.

SERVES 6

Garth Brooks
CARROT & RAISIN SALAD

At our house we've been learning that "good for you" doesn't have to mean "bad-tasting." Here's an easy side dish that comes in handy at the holiday dinner.

$^1/_2$ cup raisins

2   cups shredded carrots (4 medium)

$^1/_3$ low-fat cup yogurt

1   tablespoon honey

Combine ingredients in a small bowl. (Make sure they're mixed well.) Cover and chill.

SERVES 4-6

Jeff Carson

CHRISTMAS CARAMEL CORN

We love having people stop by the house for the holidays, so my mom makes up bowls of her famous caramel corn to encourage visitors throughout the Christmas season!

$^3/_4$ cup popping corn (makes 16 cups)

2 cups brown sugar

2 sticks oleo

$^1/_2$ cup white corn syrup

1 teaspoon salt

$^1/_2$ teaspoon baking soda

1 teaspoon butter flavoring

Preheat oven to 250° F.

Pop corn and sort out unpopped kernels. In a saucepan, combine brown sugar, oleo, corn syrup, and salt. Boil 5 minutes. Stir in soda and butter flavoring.

Pour sugar mixture immediately over popped corn. Put in 1 or 2 large flat pans. Bake for one hour. Stir every 15 minutes.

Peanuts may be added just before placing in oven. Store after cooling in a tightly covered container.

Skeeter Davis
CHRISTMAS STUFFING

During a trip to Africa I was given a party by my hosts in Nigeria. When I was told that a goat had been sacrificed in my honor, something in my spirit changed. I became a vegetarian. Here's my special Christmas stuffing—we call it dressing. My family has always wondered what made my dressing taste so special and different. Now they'll know: It's the apple!

    2   8-oz. bags herb-seasoned stuffing (1 bag cubes, 1 bag crumbs)
    3   cups water
    1   stick butter or margarine
    1   medium onion, diced
    2   medium Granny Smith apples, peeled and diced
        Sage, to taste

Preheat oven to 400° F.

Put stuffing in large mixing bowl. Boil the water and butter, then add to stuffing. Add onion, apples, sage, and mix well. Put into 9 x 13 lightly greased baking dish and bake for 30 minutes.

SERVES 6 - 8

Emilio

MRS. NAVAIRA'S CARNE GUISADA

Our family's Christmas table is unbelievable, since food is a very important part of our tradition. The banquet often continues for days and is complete with both Spanish and traditional North American dishes. We have turkey, ham, dressing, and mashed potatoes, sitting next to special "good luck" bowls of black beans, tamales, and my mother's Carne Guisada. Everybody eats, everybody laughs, everybody has a good time. Nobody ever stays away.

1 lb. round steak ($^1/_2$-inch cube size)
1 tablespoon flour
$^1/_4$ cup chopped onion
$^1/_4$ cup chopped green pepper
2 cups hot water
1 teaspoon ground cumin
1 teaspoon garlic, chopped

Fry the round steak until brown, add flour, onion, green pepper, and sauté a few more minutes. Add the water, cumin, and garlic. Cover and cook at medium heat for 15 to 20 minutes. Serve with homemade pinto beans and mashed potatoes.

SERVES 4

Donna Fargo
CHRISTMAS MUFFINS

After eating all the rich holiday cakes, cookies, and candies, I try to get back to something healthy. These muffins taste almost too good to be good for you, but they are! Try them with your favorite jelly, applesauce, apple butter, or honey.

$2^1/_2$ cups oat bran

$^1/_2$ cup brown sugar

2 teaspoons cinnamon

1 tablespoon baking powder

$^1/_2$ cup chopped walnuts

$^1/_2$ cup raisins

$^1/_2$ cup skim milk or
evaporated skim milk

$^3/_4$ cup frozen apple-juice
concentrate

2 egg whites

2 tablespoons vegetable oil

1 medium apple, cored and
chopped

Grated peel from 1 small
orange

Preheat oven to 425° F.

Mix the dry ingredients in a large bowl. Mix the milk, apple-juice concentrate, egg whites, and oil in a bowl or blender. Add to the dry ingredients and mix. Add chopped apple and grated orange peel. Line the muffin pans with paper baking cups and fill with batter. Bake for 17 to 20 minutes. Cool and store in a large plastic bag to retain moisture and softness.

SERVES 12

Tom T. Hall
APPLE SALAD

Every holiday my wife, Dixie, and I entertain at Fox Hollow, our home south of Nashville. This salad is a seasonal favorite of ours.

2   *crisp Delicious apples, cored and diced*
    Chopped cashews, pecans, or walnuts
    Small bunch seedless grapes, halved (can substitute raisins, or
        mandarin orange pieces)
1   *stalk celery, chopped (optional)*
    A poppy seed dressing, to taste

Combine the apples, nuts, grapes, celery, and dressing in bowl. Cover and chill.

SERVES 4

Wade Hayes
MOM'S BROCCOLI CASSEROLE

Everybody looks forward to my mother's cooking, especially her pecan pies, fruit salad, and broccoli casserole. Her broccoli casserole has to be good, because I've loved it since I was a kid.

$^1/_2$ cup chopped celery
$^1/_2$ cup chopped onion
$^2/_3$ tablespoon margarine
1 10-oz. package frozen chopped broccoli
1 can chicken mushroom soup
1 cup cooked rice
1 8-oz. jar Cheez Whiz

Preheat oven to 350° F.

Sauté celery and onion in margarine. Cook broccoli as per instructions on package. Mix together celery, onion, soup, rice, and Cheez Whiz. Add broccoli and pour into 9 x 13 casserole dish. Bake for 30 minutes.

SERVES 6

Hal Ketchum

LEMON-GARLIC CHICKEN

I don't pretend to be a cook, so I'll share the recipe for one of my favorite meals during any season: my wife Terrell's Lemon-Garlic Chicken. Terrell says that if everyone's on a diet, this recipe will serve six people. Otherwise, count on serving four.

LEMON-GARLIC BASTING MIXTURE

Juice of 1 lemon

1/4 cup olive oil

4 crushed garlic cloves
   (or 3 cloves)

1 teaspoon ground thyme

1 teaspoon ground black
   pepper

1 teaspoon hot sauce

6 chicken breasts, with skin and bone
Flour
Olive oil

Preheat oven to 350° F.

Mix basting ingredients in bowl. Lightly dust the chicken with flour and bake 30 minutes in a pan coated with olive oil. Remove chicken, turn, and baste with Lemon-Garlic Basting Mixture. Return to oven and bake an additional 15 minutes.

SERVES 4 - 6

Chris LeDoux

HOLIDAY MEXICAN DIP

It's a good thing cowboys aren't expected to be great chefs! A few years ago I hurriedly put together a dip to take over to my in-laws' house on Christmas Eve. Every year since then I've received a call from one family member or another, saying, "Chris, don't forget the dip." It's become my little contribution to the holiday menu.

In a large saucepan, melt a large container of Velveeta slowly.
Add:

3 *medium tomatoes, chopped fine*
2 *slices of onion, chopped fine*
1 *3-oz. can diced green chilies*
Chopped pickled jalapeño peppers to taste (be careful!)

Serve warm with tortilla chips.

SERVES 1 WHOLE CROWD
(OR $1/2$ POSSE)

Patty Loveless
SPICY
CHRISTMAS HAM

Most Southerners include ham as part of the Christmas dinner. Here's a great holiday ham recipe you can try. If you like, you can add potatoes, carrots, or turnips thirty minutes before the ham is cooked to give the vegetables a nice spicy taste as well.

  5 lb. ham
  1 tablespoon whole cloves
2$^1/_2$ quarts apple cider
 $^1/_2$ teaspoon ground allspice
 $^1/_4$ teaspoon ground cinnamon (or you can use 2 cinnamon sticks)

Push the cloves into the fat layer around the rind of the ham. Put the ham into a large Dutch oven. Add the spices to the cider and pour over the ham. Cover and heat until the liquid is boiling. Reduce the heat and let simmer for 1$^1/_2$ to 2 hours, or until the ham is tender.

S E R V E S   8 - 1 0

Barbara Mandrell

MARY MANDRELL'S CORN PUDDING

At Christmas the whole family always looks forward to my mom's delicious corn pudding.

2 tablespoons butter or margarine

1 onion, chopped

2 cans (15¼ oz each) corn, drained and patted dry with paper towel

2 tablespoons cornmeal

2 tablespoons all-purpose flour

3 cups half-and-half

4 eggs

2 tablespoons fresh parsley, chopped

1 teaspoon Worcestershire sauce

¼ teaspoon mustard powder

¾ teaspoon salt

¼ teaspoon cayenne pepper

Position rack in center of oven and preheat to 350° F. Butter shallow 2-quart baking dish. In skillet, melt butter over medium heat. Add onion; cook until softened, about 5 minutes. In baking dish, combine corn, cornmeal, flour, and onion and butter mixture. In bowl, combine half-and-half, eggs, parsley, Worcestershire sauce, mustard powder, salt, and cayenne; stir into corn mixture. Place large roasting pan in center of oven rack. Place baking dish in pan. Fill roasting pan with water, halfway up sides of baking dish. Bake until center of pudding is just set and top is golden, 45 to 55 minutes. Cool in roasting pan 10 minutes. Remove from water and serve.

SERVES 8

Martina McBride
Tortilla Soup

This soup will warm you up on those cold December nights.

1 large onion, sliced	8 cups chicken broth
8 cloves garlic, minced	Salt and pepper to taste
1/4 cup vegetable oil	Vegetable oil for frying
7 green chilies, stemmed, seeded	12 corn tortillas, cut into strips
4 cups water	1 1/2 cups shredded Monterey Jack cheese
5 tomatoes, seeded, chopped	
2 tablespoons vegetable oil	2 avocados, cut into wedges

Add onion and garlic to oil in stockpot. Cook over medium heat until tender, stirring constantly; increase heat. Add chilies. Cook for 1 minute or until tender, stirring constantly. Remove 1 chile and cut into 10 strips; set aside. Add water and tomatoes to stockpot. Bring to a boil. Simmer for 30 minutes. Puree in blender in batches. Heat 2 tablespoons oil in stockpot over medium heat until hot but not smoking. Add pureed mixture. Cook for 5 minutes, stirring constantly. Stir in chicken broth and salt and pepper. Simmer for 15 minutes. Heat 1/2 inch of oil in skillet over high heat until hot but not smoking. Fry tortilla strips in batches for 30 seconds, stirring constantly. Drain on paper towels. Place equal portions of tortilla strips in 10 heated bowls. Pour soup over tortillas. Top with chile strips. Sprinkle with cheese and garnish with avocado wedges.

SERVES 10

$\mathcal{D}$ean $\mathcal{M}$iller
CHRISTMAS CRANBERRY PUNCH

My idea of cooking is to throw some nachos on a plate, add cheese, and microwave. So I don't spend much time in the kitchen, but I like to visit people who do. One friend serves this Christmas punch every holiday season. It's very tasty, and she says it's easy to make.

$^2/_3$ cup sugar

1 5-inch cinnamon stick,
     broken into small pieces

2 teaspoons whole allspice

2 whole cloves

$^1/_4$ teaspoon salt

4 cups cranberry juice
     cocktail

$2^1/_2$ cups unsweetened pineapple
     juice

   Ice ring

$3^1/_2$ cups chilled ginger ale

   Orange and/or lime slices,
     optional

Mix together sugar, spices, salt, cranberry juice, and pineapple juice in a large cooking pot. Cover and simmer approximately 10 minutes. Strain and chill. To serve, pour chilled punch over ice ring in punch bowl and carefully pour ginger ale down the side of the bowl. Add orange or lime slices to float on the top.

SERVES 15
($^1/_2$ CUP EACH)

Mark Miller
SHRIMP KABOBS

Moving from Ohio to Florida ended many traditions for my family, but it also started some new ones. Shrimp has become part of our holiday menu, even though we're now living in landlocked Tennessee. These kabobs are great on the day following the big Christmas dinner.

$1^1/_3$ cups soy sauce

$^2/_3$ cup lemon juice

  1 small onion, minced

  1 clove garlic, minced

$2^1/_2$ pounds shrimp, peeled and deveined

12 cherry tomatoes

  1 large green pepper, cut into chunks

Prepare a marinade with the soy sauce, lemon juice, onion, and garlic. Marinate shrimp for approximately $2^1/_2$ hours in the refrigerator. Place shrimps, tomatoes, and green pepper chunks on skewers and broil for ten minutes, turning several times.

SERVES 6

Ronnie Milsap
ENGLISH TRIFLE

Ifirst heard about this dessert when I toured England with Glen Campbell in 1977. At a London restaurant, our waiter asked if we wanted "trifle." I admitted that I'd never even heard of it. I have never in my life tasted a better dessert. Each year, our British friend Joan Cook arrives on Christmas Eve with a huge glass bowl filled with trifle.

2 3-oz. jelly rolls
1 6-oz. package Jell-O (raspberry or strawberry)
1 8-oz. can fruit cocktail, drained

1 package Bird's Custard Powder
1/2 pint whipping cream
Chocolate sprinkles (to decorate)

Cut jelly rolls into slices and place in a single layer in the bottom of a very large glass bowl. Make up the Jell-O according to directions and while it's still hot, pour over jelly rolls. Add fruit cocktail. Refrigerate until Jell-O sets (3 or more hours).

When Jell-O has set, make up custard according to directions and pour over Jell-O. Allow to cool down and thicken, approximately 1 hour. Make up whipped cream and put a layer over custard. Scatter chocolate sprinkles over cream to decorate.

SERVES 8

Jimmy C. Newman

CAJUN RICE DRESSING

No Cajun Christmas dinner is complete without Cajun Rice Dressing. This is a recipe that my wife, Mae, has been fixing for years. She says you can leave out the parsley and bell pepper if you wish.

6 pork chops	cup dried bell pepper
1/4 lb. fresh liver	6 cups cooked white rice
1 large onion, chopped	1 cup green onion, diced
	1 cup parsley, diced

Salt, pepper, and red pepper

Put pork chops, liver, onion, and bell pepper in pot. Season with salt and peppers to taste. Cover completely with water. Cook over low heat for 1 hour with lid on. If the water cooks away, add more after cooking an hour and let it cook down until brown. (Check bottom of the pot frequently for sticking.) Add more water (about 1 1/2 cups) and simmer for 15 minutes. Take meats out of liquid. Debone pork chops. Grind or mince to a coarse texture. Put ground meat in large bowl. Add cooked rice to meat mixture. Add green onion and parsley. Now add the liquid to your mixture. (Not too much!) Cover bowl (to keep warm) and let sit for 25 to 30 minutes. Serve hot.

SERVES 6 - 8

Stella Parton
MAMA'S FRIED TATERS

Rituals are important to me, no matter how simple or extensive they are. One fun tradition that I've kept up over the years is serving Mama's Fried Taters on Christmas morning, made especially for my son, Tim. This really is Mama's recipe, but I added Italian seasoning as my own twist. This recipe was taken from *Stella Parton's Country Cookin'*.

6 *medium potatoes*
$^1/_2$ *cup safflower oil*
   Salt and pepper to taste
1 *large onion, chopped*
1 *red pepper, diced*
1 *green pepper, diced*

Peel potatoes and slice thin. Heat oil in large skillet over medium heat. Add potatoes. Add salt and pepper. Cook uncovered on medium heat for 12 to 15 minutes. Add onion, red and green pepper, and cook for an additional 7 minutes. Cover and let steam for 5 minutes. Remove lid and let potatoes brown. Cook until tender. Optional: Add 1 tablespoon Italian seasoning.

SERVES 6

Gretchen Peters

EGGNOG FRENCH TOAST

Inade this for breakfast last Christmas morning and everyone raved. It sounds a little odd but it's delicious. And for those people who like the *idea* of eggnog better than they enjoy drinking it, this is the perfect way to get your yearly quota, *and* get rid of the leftover eggnog!

2   cups eggnog
1   egg, slightly beaten
$\frac{1}{2}$ cup cinnamon
3   tablespoons butter
6   large slices French bread

Mix eggnog, egg, and cinnamon in a shallow bowl, stirring well. Melt 1 tablespoon butter in a skillet or on a griddle. Dip French bread in batter and place on griddle. Cook on each side for 1 to $1\frac{1}{2}$ minutes, or until golden brown. Use remaining butter as needed. Serve warm with heated maple syrup.

SERVES 6

Jeanne Pruett
SWEET POTATO CASSEROLE

I'm the best cook that I've ever known, and I take great pride in this fact. Here's a family favorite from one of my *Feedin' Friends* cookbooks; this dish is a must at every Christmas dinner. Try it yourself and then look me in the eye and tell me it's not wonderful!

  3   cups raw grated sweet potatoes
1 1/2 cups sugar
  1   stick butter
 3/4 cup buttermilk
  1   cup chopped pecans
 1/2 teaspoon ground cloves
  1   teaspoon cinnamon
  2   eggs, beaten

Preheat oven to 300° F.

In a large mixing bowl, mix all ingredients. Save eggs until last and blend slowly into mixture. Place in casserole dish and bake 1 1/4 hours.

SERVES 6 - 8

Collin Raye

ITALIAN-STYLE POT ROAST

More than any other food, I love pot roast. That's what I always ask for during the holidays or any other time. I especially like roast that makes a great late-night sandwich, like this recipe does.

1/4 cup chopped prosciutto	2 tablespoons cooking oil
1 large onion, chopped	4 lb. beef chuck roast
4 stalks celery, chopped	1/2 teaspoon pepper
1 clove garlic, finely chopped	1 cup beef consommé
1 tablespoon butter or margarine	3 bay leaves
	1 1/2 cups water
	1 clove garlic

Preheat oven to 275° F.

Sauté prosciutto, onion, celery, and garlic in butter until onion is translucent, and set aside. Heat oil in 5-quart roasting pan and brown meat on all sides. Pepper all sides of meat; add consommé and bay leaves and cook, covered, in a slow oven for 1 hour, checking to see the consommé does not cook away. Remove from oven. Add water and prosciutto mixture. Bake an additional 2 1/2 hours or until meat is fork-tender.

SERVES 4

Johnny Russell
CHICKEN & DUMPLINGS

On Christmas day we always had a big dinner. Everything my mother cooked tasted wonderful. We never had turkey because the family preferred chicken. So Mother always cooked chicken and dumplings.

2¹/₂ pound fryer
1¹/₂ teaspoon salt
2 cups sifted flour
¹/₄ teaspoon pepper
¹/₂ stick margarine

Cut chicken into pieces and put into a large pot. Cover with water and add 1 teaspoon salt. Simmer until chicken is tender. Remove skin and bones, saving the broth. Put flour into bowl, add ¹/₂ teaspoon salt, and 1 cup broth. Stir until lumps are all gone, then knead on floured board. Add more flour if dough is sticky. Divide dough into 4 pieces and roll each piece out thin. Cut into squares. Bring remaining broth to a boil and drop in the squares, one at a time. Add water or bouillon if needed. When all squares are added to broth, cover and turn down heat. Simmer 10 or 12 minutes. Add pepper and margarine. Add cooked chicken pieces.

SERVES 6 - 8

Daryle Singletary
SOUTHERN PECAN PIE

One of my favorite holiday desserts is pecan pie. Christmas dinner wouldn't be the same without it.

$^1/_2$ cup firmly packed brown sugar

$1^1/_2$ teaspoons all-purpose flour

3 eggs, beaten

$1^1/_4$ cups light corn syrup

$1^1/_2$ teaspoons vanilla

2 tablespoons butter or margarine

1 cup pecan chips
    Prepared pie shell

Preheat oven to 375° F.

In a large bowl, mix brown sugar, flour, eggs, corn syrup, and vanilla. Stir in butter and pecans. Put into prepared pie shell and bake for 40 to 50 minutes, or until the middle of the pie is browned. (One great variation is to stir a teaspoon of grated orange rind into the pecan and butter mixture.) Let cool before serving.

SERVES 8

Connie Smith
STRAWBERRY CAKE

Years ago I bought a birthday card for my daughter, and on that card was a recipe for Strawberry Cake. Over the years I changed the recipe and now it's definitely mine! Every Christmas I bake a Strawberry Cake for my family, a friend, or a neighbor.

1 package white cake mix	1 cup salad oil
2$^1/_2$ tablespoons flour	3 large eggs (or 4 medium)
1 small package strawberry Jell-O	$^1/_2$ cup cold water
	$^1/_2$ small package frozen strawberries (thawed)

Preheat oven to 350° F.

Combine the cake mix, flour, and Jell-O. Add the oil and then beat in the eggs. Add the water and the strawberries. Mix it up. Bake the cake in a Bundt cake pan (greased and floured) for 40 to 50 minutes.

Icing: I don't really follow a recipe for the icing. I just mix a little strawberry juice and melted butter with some powdered (confectioner's) sugar until it looks like it will run down the cake without being too runny!

SERVES 12

Pam Tillis
SWEET POTATO BISCUITS

There's nothing like biscuits served with honey on a cold Christmas morning. Sweet potatoes make this recipe something special.

- 2 cups all-purpose flour
- 2 teaspoons baking powder
- 1¹/₂ tablespoons light brown sugar
- ¹/₄ teaspoon salt
- ³/₄ cup shortening
- 1 cup mashed sweet potatoes (cooked)
  Buttermilk

Preheat oven to 425°F.

Sift flour, baking powder, brown sugar, and salt into bowl. Cut in shortening until crumbly. Add sweet potatoes. Mix, adding buttermilk for proper rolling consistency. Roll ¹/₂ inch thick on lightly floured board. Cut biscuits with cutter or glass and place on greased baking sheet. Bake for 15 minutes or until golden brown.

SERVES 12

Aaron Tippin

AARON'S MEXICAN CASSEROLE

This recipe serves four unless one of the people at the table is me. Then it'll serve three! My wife, Thea, and I consider this casserole one of our favorite holiday dishes.

1 lb. lean ground beef
1 medium yellow onion, chopped
1 package taco seasoning
1 package corn tortillas
2 4-oz. cans Mexican-flavored pinto beans
1 8-oz. package shredded cheddar cheese

Preheat oven to 350° F.

Brown meat and onion. Add taco seasoning and water as per directions on package. Let simmer for five minutes.

In casserole dish put one layer of corn tortillas, then spoon meat mixture on top. Spoon on layer of beans and put on layer of cheese. Repeat until you run out of ingredients, ending with cheese. Bake for 30 minutes.

SERVES 4

Tanya Tucker
CHRISTMAS EGGNOG

I love to cook and I love to entertain, so I'm constantly asking friends and family to my home during the holiday season. Eggnog has become as much a part of our celebration as the Christmas tree!

    6 eggs, separated
 1/3 cup sugar
    5 cups milk
    2 teaspoons rum extract
    1 teaspoon vanilla
    1 cup whipped cream
       Nutmeg

In large bowl, beat egg whites until peaks form. Add yolks and sugar. Beat well. Stir in milk, rum extract, and vanilla. Allow the mixture to chill. Before serving, fold in the whipped cream. Sprinkle with nutmeg.

SERVES 16
(1/2 CUP EACH)

Steve Wariner

Oatmeal Refrigerator Cookies

Every Christmas I bake these cookies with my sons, Ross and Ryan. We have fun, and we always clean up afterward. However, my wife, Caryn, has to remove flour from the ceiling and other odd places!

1 cup shortening	2 teaspoons vanilla
1 cup sugar	1¹/₂ cups sifted flour
1 cup brown sugar, firmly packed	1 teaspoon baking soda
	¹/₂ teaspoon salt
2 eggs, well beaten	3 cups quick-cooking oats

Preheat oven to 400° F.

Cream together shortening and sugars until light and fluffy. Add eggs, one at a time, beating well after each addition. Blend in vanilla. Sift together flour, baking soda, and salt. Gradually add dry ingredients to creamed mixture; mix well. Stir in oats.

Divide dough in thirds. Shape in 10" x 1¹/₄" rolls. Wrap tightly in plastic wrap or waxed paper. Chill several hours or overnight.

Cut rolls into thin slices. Place about 1¹/₂" apart on ungreased baking sheets. Bake 6 to 8 minutes or until done. Remove from baking sheets. Cool on racks. Makes 8 dozen.

SERVES SANTA & HIS ELVES

Bryan White

GRANDMA WHITE'S PEANUT BUTTER FUDGE

These days my mother and I have developed a new tradition. We spend time renting movies, eating junk food, and catching up on our long talks. But it's Grandma White's cooking that takes center stage each Christmas. During the holidays, even my friends stop by, hoping Grandma will ask if anyone is hungry for peanut butter fudge.

3 cups sugar
3/4 stick butter or margarine
1 cup of milk (condensed milk can be substituted but fudge will not set as well)
1 teaspoon vanilla

Heat the above to a boil, stirring constantly. Cook to soft ball stage, approximately 5 minutes. Let set at room temperature and cut into squares when cool.

While still hot, add:
1 cup chopped pecans or walnuts
1 12-oz. package peanut butter chips
1 tablespoon peanut butter
1 7-oz. jar marshmallow cream
Pour into a buttered 9 x 13 pan to set.

SERVES A FULL HOUSE

Biographies

BILL ANDERSON, who holds a journalism degree from the University of Georgia, is one of Nashville's most successful songwriters and entertainers. A former cast member on the soap *One Life to Live,* he has hosted several Nashville Network TV shows and written his autobiography, as well as several books about country music. He is a regular host of the Grand Ole Opry.

JOHN BERRY received a Grammy nomination for his number one hit, "Your Love Amazes Me." His debut album went gold, and the single was named Song of the Year by the Music City News Awards. John was a 1996 nominee for the Academy of Country Music's Male Artist of the Year.

SUZY BOGGUSS won the Country Music Association Horizon Award and Academy of Country Music's Top New Female Artist award. A platinum-selling artist and Grammy-nominated vocalist, she's known for such hits as "Aces" and "Letting Go."

GARTH BROOKS is the only male artist in the Recording Industry Association of America's (RIAA) history to have two solo albums top the ten million mark in domestic sales. Also the fastest-selling artist in RIAA history—his domestic sales are in excess of fifty-eight million—Garth is credited with bringing an entirely new generation of fans to country music.

JEFF CARSON'S second and third single releases, "Not On Your Life" and "The Car," both became number one hit songs. He was named one of the Top Ten New Male Artists of 1996 by *Country America* magazine, and his video of "The Car" received an Academy of Country Music nomination for Video of the Year.

SKEETER DAVIS began her career as one of the Davis Sisters, along with Betty Jack, who died in a car accident. Skeeter made musical history with her 1963 crossover hit "The End of the World," which is now a classic. A member of the Grand Ole Opry since 1959, Skeeter's autobiography is called *Busfare to Kentucky.* She and her band tour worldwide.

EMILIO, before achieving country music stardom, had propelled Tejano music from a regional genre to the fastest-growing form of Latin-based music in America. Emilio has been nominated for two Grammy awards and has won multiple Tejano Music Awards for Entertainer of the Year, Male Vocalist of the Year, and Album and Showband of the Year.

DONNA FARGO was the National Association of Record Merchandisers' Best-Selling Female Artist in 1972, when her blockbuster "The Happiest Girl In The Whole U.S.A." became a number one country smash, as well as a pop hit. That same year she won a Grammy and numerous country music awards, including Most Performed Song of the Year. She later had more number one records, such as "Funny Face" and "Superman."

TOM T. HALL first rose to country music prominence as a songwriter, penning such huge sellers as "Harper Valley P.T.A." and "Watermelon Wine." As an artist, he has had numerous hits and was host of *Pop Goes The Country*. His "Harper Valley P.T.A." became a television series starring Barbara Eden. Tom T. is the author of several works of fiction, as well as a songwriter's handbook.

WADE HAYES had four top ten singles during his first year as an artist, including two number ones. He was *Billboard*'s Top New Country Artist of 1995 and *Radio & Records*' 1995 New Artist MVP. In 1995, *Entertainment Tonight* named him the Hottest New Face in Country Music. His debut album was the only new artist release to be certified gold.

LOUDILLA JOHNSON represents all country music fans—the most loyal fans in the world—by being included in this book. Loudilla and her sisters, Loretta and Kay, are the founders of the International Fan Club Organization. They also started the Loretta Lynn Fan Club, which set an industry standard for star/fan organizations.

HAL KETCHUM, critically acclaimed as a singer/songwriter, released his first major label album, *Past The Point Of Rescue*, in 1991. The album's first single, "Small Town Saturday Night," became *Radio & Records*' Number One Single of the Year Nationwide. A gold-selling artist, Hal is also a Broadcast Music Inc. (BMI) award-winning writer.

CHRIS LEDOUX is not only a gold-selling country music star, he is also a world champion bronc buster, having won the gold buckle in 1976. His 1993 duet with Garth Brooks, "Whatcha Gonna Do With A Cowboy," was nominated for a Grammy as well as the Academy of Country Music and TNN/Music City News Vocal Collaboration awards.

PATTY LOVELESS began her career touring with the Wilburn Brothers. In 1995 she accomplished an astonishing feat when she was awarded the Country Music Assocation award for Album of the Year for the second time, for her album *When Fallen Angels Fly*. The only other woman to receive the award was Anne Murray, for her album *A Little Good News*.

BARBARA MANDRELL was the first artist ever to win the Country Music Association's Entertainer of the Year award for two consecutive years, 1980 and 1981. She also had her own popular television series, *Barbara Mandrell and the Mandrell Sisters*. Her autobiography, *Get to the Heart*, reached number one on *The New York Times Best Sellers* list.

MARTINA MCBRIDE, a Grammy-winner, and a platinum-selling artist, won the Country Music Association's award for 1994 Video of the Year for her release "Independence Day." The song became CMA's 1995 Song of the Year. Her latest album, *Wild Angels*, was named Country Album of the Year, and the title cut was named Video of the Year.

BOB MCDILL, whose thirty number one songs have spanned four decades, defines the art of songwriting for aspiring country writers. He has had over 350 songs recorded, and is a member of the Nashville Songwriters International Hall of Fame. His hits include "Amanda," "Good Ole Boys Like Me," and the recent Grammy-nominated "Gone Country."

DEAN MILLER has had cuts by such artists as James House, Shawn Camp, and has cowritten with House, Marty Stuart, Kostas, and many other top writers. He is currently recording an album for a major country label.

MARK MILLER went from college jock to superstar after founding Sawyer Brown. The group won CMA's Horizon Award in 1985, and had such number one hits as "Step That Step." In 1994, they were presented with the TNN/Music City Group of the Year award.

✤ 𝓑iographies ✤

RONNIE MILSAP is the second-biggest-charting country artist in *Radio & Records*' history, and *Billboard*'s 21st-biggest-selling country singles artist. Ronnie has had thirty-five number one records, has won six Grammy awards, and was the Country Music Association Entertainer of the Year in 1977.

JIMMY C. NEWMAN is the first Cajun country singer to join the Grand Ole Opry, and he has been a member since 1956. Noted for such hits as "A Fallen Star" and "Cry, Cry, Darling," Jimmy C. and his band tour extensively in Europe, the United States, and Canada.

STELLA PARTON, who has recorded fifteen albums, has expanded her career to include acting roles in such theatrical productions as *Gentlemen Prefer Blondes*. Born into a musical family, Stella tours worldwide, and has written *Stella Parton's Country Cookin'*.

GRETCHEN PETERS is the Grammy-nominated writer of "Independence Day," the Country Music Association's 1995 Song of the Year. Her 1996 highly acclaimed debut album, *The Secret Of Life*, released by Imprint Records, proves her to be a top performer as well.

JEANNE PRUETT has written songs for Marty Robbins, Conway Twitty, and Tammy Wynette. Her crossover hit "Satin Sheets" won her *Billboard*'s Album of the Year award. An Opry regular, Jeanne opened a restaurant, Feedin' Friends, at Opryland.

COLLIN RAYE is considered one of the industry's finest vocalists and stylists. Since the release of his groundbreaking song, "Love, Me," Collin has had four platinum albums, seven number one singles, fourteen top five singles, and nine number one videos.

JOHNNY RUSSELL combines songwriting, singing, and comedy. His song "Act Naturally," a hit for both Buck Owens and the Beatles, was recently re-released on the Beatles' *Help* CD. In 1985, Johnny joined the Grand Ole Opry, where his humor and storytelling ability keep him in demand as a host, as well as performer.

DARYLE SINGLETARY released his critically acclaimed debut album in 1995. It has netted him two top five singles, two top five videos, and the full attention of the country music industry. Daryle was discovered by superstar Randy Travis, who also produced his first album. *Country America* named Daryle among its Top Ten New Stars of 1996.

CONNIE SMITH burst upon the country music scene in the 1960s when her classic hit "Once A Day" stayed at number one in *Billboard* for ten weeks. A member of the Grand Ole Opry, Connie has recorded more than forty albums. Her latest album is on Warner Brothers.

PAM TILLIS is the daughter of country legend Mel Tillis. She found stardom in 1990, after establishing herself as one of Nashville's premier songwriters. In 1994, she became the Country Music Association's Female Vocalist of the Year. Her platinum-selling hits include "Don't Tell Me What To Do," "When You Walk In The Room," and "Mi Vida Loca."

AARON TIPPIN was a noted songwriter when he signed a major label contract in 1990. His debut single, "You've Got To Stand For Something," rocketed him to stardom. Later hits, such as "I Wouldn't Have It Any Other Way," have moved him into platinum sales status.

TANYA TUCKER had her first hit with "Delta Dawn" at age thirteen. By age fifteen she had a Grammy nomination, a gold record, and had made the cover of *Rolling Stone* magazine. She is one of the top five women in country music to have the greatest number of top-ten records. In 1991 she was the Country Music Association's Female Artist of the Year.

STEVE WARINER, guitarist, singer, and songwriter, was discovered by Dottie West in 1972. Steve had his first number one single in 1976, with "All Roads Lead To You." He won a Grammy for his collaboration track, "Restless," with Mark O'Connor and Ricky Scaggs.

BRYAN WHITE is country music's newest and youngest star. At age twenty-two he is already a gold-selling artist with two number one hits. Bryan was named Country Music Television's Rising Star for the network's 1995 year-end video countdown.